Food
❧ Combining ❧

Food Combining

Peter and Donna Thomson

BLOOMSBURY

First published in 1996 by
Bloomsbury Publishing plc
38 Soho Square
London W1V 5DF

This edition first published in 1997

A copy of the CIP entry for this book is available from the British Library

ISBN 0 7475 3300 8

10 9 8 7 6 5 4 3 2 1

Designed by Hugh Adams, AB3, London
Typeset by Hewer Text Composition Services, Edinburgh
Printed and bound in Great Britain by Clays Ltd, St Ives plc

CONTENTS

————

Contents

Contents

Contents

Contents

Contents

PART 1
Food Combining Will Work for You

❦ CHAPTER 1 ❦

The Good News about Food Combining

• The Golden Rule

There is only one basic rule: *Don't mix starch meals with protein meals*.

Food combining is *the* healthy diet for the 21st century.

• The Feel-Good Factor •

Food combining assumes that people are mentally alert, physically fit, able to cope with stress and resistant to disease. It expects this to be the natural state, without the intervention of the doctor or of medicines.

Food combining is a diet based on the observations and experience of people in the real world, not an attempt to force people into the straitjacket of untested theory. A long-term study of diet-related disease coordinated by the Institute of Nutrition in Rome identified the people of the village of Celso, on its hilltop, as those least likely to die of diet-related disease. Most of their meals are based on home-made pasta, bread, soup, fruit, vegetables and olive oil, and include a glass of red wine. Protein is not normally eaten with their starch- and vegetable-based meals.

3

The scientific explanation of why food combining works starts with the real world, with the observation that it is a diet that works! The scientists are slowly beginning to explain just why food combining is such a successful diet.

But there is only one way to put food combining to the test – try it!

• Why the Food Combining Lifestyle is Easy •

The main guidelines of food combining are:

- Don't mix starch meals with protein meals (see page 25).

- No more than one protein meal each day (see page 27).

- Eat some foods high in potassium and calcium every day (see page 29).

- Women who are not very active may prefer to eat one starch meal, one fruit meal and one protein meal each day (see page 30).

- Men may need extra energy and require two starch meals a day (see page 30).

- Fill up on starchy foods: satisfy your appetite with bread, rice, potatoes and pasta, all of which contain easily accessible energy and are also rich in fibre. Choose wholemeal foods when you can. Eat wholegrain cereals, not highly refined flour (see page 26).

- Eat plenty of non-starchy vegetables – as much as you like (see page 30)!

- Eat plenty of fresh fruit – as much as you like (see page 31)!

- Eat a wide variety of fruit and vegetables (see page 30).

- Use olive oil if you need oil for cooking or dressings (see page 31).

- Eat butter and cream in moderation (see page 31).

- Don't add sugar (see page 32).

- Don't eat foods made from mixtures of fat and sugar, such as biscuits and cakes (see page 42).

- Don't smother starch meals in fat (see page 32).

- Don't add extra salt (see page 32).

- Take gentle exercise, which helps digestion (see page 34–5).

• Why Food Combining is Inexpensive •

The food combining lifestyle encourages us to dispense with expensive junk and convenience foods.

Until recently, almost all meals were cooked from fresh ingredients. We ate fresh vegetables in season. Some were tinned, but many housewives scorned the use of tinned vegetables and used only those grown in their own gardens or bought from the local greengrocer. These in turn came from local producers and were used before they had time to lose many of their vitamins. Tinned fish and meat, although available, were similarly used less often than fresh by those who valued a healthy lifestyle.

Nowadays, many people eat convenience foods, such as dehydrated, chilled or frozen ready-prepared meals. Frozen, pre-cooked chips are used instead of making fresh ones and we can even buy ready-prepared baked potatoes. Many of us have been persuaded that it is easier to heat up a plastic pack of chilli con carne than make our own, and we will cheerfully serve our families with tubs of coloured goo as desserts, rather than give them a fresh apple or banana.

Many such convenience foods are treated with preservatives, colourings and artificial flavourings, none of them nutritionally valuable and many highly suspect. Conditions such as hyperactivity in children may result from some of these. Many more convenience foods are contaminated by the addition of high levels of sugar and/or other sweeteners, which are again empty of nutrition and may be positively harmful. Many people are uncomfortably aware of this trap and yet uncertain how to escape from it.

The food combining lifestyle will help anyone who wants to feed themselves and their family nourishing food, yet needs to watch the cost. All you need do is use *only* fresh or pure frozen ingredients – nothing pre-packed or processed and refined. In this way you will know exactly what your family is eating and that you are taking in no harmful additives.

And you will find that the shopping basket filled with fresh vegetables and fruit is less expensive than that crammed with packets of ready-cooked convenience meals. Compare the price of a bag of potatoes in the supermarket with a single baked potato from a take-away, or the price of a packet of spaghetti with the much smaller amount in a small tin of the same. You are no longer paying for flavourings, colourings or packaging, nor for someone else's wages in the factories in which such meals are prepared. You are simply paying for fresh, wholesome food.

Compare the prices of natural foods with those of ready-made foods. Why buy your family cakes, for instance, when a bowl of fruit will cost no more and do them far more good? Why buy meat pies and frozen chips – not a food-combining recommendation anyway – when fresh meat and vegetables will be cheaper and healthier? Why buy fish fingers, smothered in breadcrumbs and colouring, when fish such as coley can be bought inexpensively?

Not only will your family be fitter following this lifestyle, but they will not suffer the between-meal hunger pangs and cravings that they probably experience on a 'normal' diet. This is because the digestive system is working at its correct pace, with none of the highs and lows of blood-sugar level that are part of the pattern of 'convenience food' eating, and the food is taking longer to pass through. Our bodies are more satisfied on the food combining lifestyle and snacks such as cakes, biscuits, crisps and chocolate bars are no longer wanted. If you have not eaten enough at one meal to satisfy you until the next, you can sustain your body with a snack of a few nuts or some fresh or dried fruit.

Snacks are among the most expensive, and the most unhealthy, items in many Western diets, yet there are few people, even those on the lowest of incomes, who do without them. Leave them out of your shopping basket and you will have more money to buy the more nutritious vegetables and fruit that are recommended as a large part of the food combining lifestyle.

• Why the Food Combining Lifestyle Saves Time •

Many people say they rely on convenience foods because they have no time to prepare fresh foods, and it is true that the pace of life is faster nowadays. But in fact, cooking fresh vegetables and preparing fresh fruit often takes less of our time than preparing so-called convenience foods.

We probably have more spare time now than any of our ancestors ever had. We work shorter hours – it is not so many years since a 12-hour day was the norm – and we spend much more time on leisure pursuits, many of them, such as watching television, in our own homes.

Preparing our own meals is a satisfying and relaxing activity, which can be shared by all members of the family. Children can help, especially with such tasks as shelling peas and beans, or scrubbing the skins of potatoes. And there are a great many meals that can be quickly prepared and then left to cook themselves. You will find many such recipes in this book.

Many people on low incomes have decided that their children need a parent at home, or they may have more time because of unemployment. For such people the food combining lifestyle makes ideal use of their time and is an excellent way to feed families cheaply, nutritiously and healthily. Kitchen appliances such as a pressure cooker and a microwave oven will help save money on the cooking, so these methods are recommended, but all the recipes in this book can be used by those who do not have such appliances.

Time need be no bar to following the food combining lifestyle, and it will have the great benefit of making you and your family fitter and healthier. And this, in turn, will save time.

• Don't Be Dominated by Your Diet •

Every meal you enjoy that follows this lifestyle helps to keep you fit and healthy, but you don't have to follow it like a slave.

- You don't have to count calories – unless you want to.

- You don't have to understand the history of the diet, although it makes a fascinating story.

- You don't have to understand modern science to discover that today's doctors and research scientists are finding that this lifestyle, based on traditional ways of eating, is better than many of their expensive pills and potions at fighting cancer, heart disease, digestive disorders and many other ailments of our modern society.

- You don't have to give up any of the food ingredients that you like – although you may find yourself eating them at different meals.

- When you eat out, follow your lifestyle if you can, but it doesn't matter occasionally if you don't.

❦ CHAPTER 2 ❦
Why Science and Medicine Support Food Combining

• The History of Food Combining •

Since the dawn of medical history, with the ancient Greeks, there have been reports of the ways in which food can cause and cure illness. But the main tradition of Western medicine held that food cannot cause disease, and unquestioned tradition is very hard to shift.

Dr William Howard Hay (1866–1940) managed to question this tradition more than most, but he was just one of many who questioned the relationship between what what we eat and our physical and mental health. Dr Rollier of Leysin, Switzerland, Dr Rasmus Alsaker and Dr J. H. Tilden of Denver were others who questioned the fashion for refined foods and asked whether they could be the cause of a rising tide of new diseases sweeping the world.

Dr Hay treated his patients according to medical tradition for the first 16 years of his practice, until his own ill health caused him to re-evaluate his approach to medicine. He had also observed his patients suffering from increased ill health between 1891 and 1911, with more heart disease, circulatory disease, digestive disorders and cancers.

When he became seriously ill, he deduced that the only cause of this increase in disease, which was common to all his patients, was the increase in protein and refined food in their diet. He decided that the only cure for his own ill health was to change his pattern of eating back to a more natural lifestyle, contrary to the conventional view at that time, which held that diet played little part in health and that medicines were needed to correct these ailments.

Dr Hay, and others like him, became convinced that these diseases could easily be prevented, and indeed cured, by following a more natural lifestyle. He studied all the food science available to him and constructed his now famous diet. He was the first person to benefit from his own improved lifestyle. He followed the food combining diet that he devised himself and impressed his fellow doctors with his rapid recovery. He then put this practical experience to good use.

One report that strongly influenced Dr Hay was that of Dr Robert McCarrison, an officer in the British Army medical services, who observed extreme longevity in the Himalayas. The population there subsisted on nuts, vegetables and fruit, mostly raw, wholegrain bread, with small amounts of milk and cheese. McCarrison also observed that these people suffered very little disease, unlike the Europeans, who imported their refined diets with them.

Dr Hay treated a large number of people, with a wide range of chronic illnesses. He observed from his own practical experience and observation that many of these people, written off as incurable by their own doctors, recovered and then maintained good health when following his diet.

He was appointed director of the Sun-Diet Health Foundation in 1927. The president of this foundation, at the age of 68, based his own good health on the exercise that he took – skipping with a rope 200 times, always running upstairs, and walking four to five miles each day. He ate no breakfast, drank a pint of milk and a pint of orange juice for his lunch, and at night had a meal of salad, broth, cooked vegetables and the occasional dessert.

By 1935 Dr Hay was medical director of Hay System Inc. and set out his ideas in *A New Health Era*. Some of his ideas have not stood the test of time – he was not aware of the nature of smallpox and thought all disease might be caused by diet or living conditions – and our own knowledge of the internal workings of the human body has progressed a long way since he wrote the book. But in spite of this, his observations on diet and health remain an accurate basis for a healthy lifestyle.

• Why Science Supports Food Combining •

At long last the weight of medical and scientific opinion is agreeing with Dr Hay. Unfortunately the legacy of old textbooks and a huge processed-food industry combined with a recent tradition of indulging in cakes, pies and puddings, has slowed down progress.

The results of the latest medical research are as follows:

- The most dramatic revelation of modern science is that lysine, an essential component of protein, is destroyed if proteins and starches are cooked together. Similar processes take place in our digestive system. So keep starch and protein separate!

Other medical research has concentrated on regions where diet-related disease is particularly rare.

- The Cretans' traditional food is rich in grains, vegetables and fruit, with a moderate amount of fish and cheese. They eat some poultry but little red meat. Olive oil is the main source of fat in their diet. Walnuts and purslane are thought to make a significant contribution to their low rate of heart attacks.

- In a recent medical study heart patients were advised to eat like Cretans. These patients were found to have a better chance of survival than those who follow the low-cholesterol diet recommended by the American Heart Association.

- Diabetes has now reached epidemic proportions and coronary artery disease is also increasing among Pacific islanders who have adopted a sedentary lifestyle and a diet rich in Western-style junk food.

11

- A diet rich in starch, not just fibre, may be a major protective factor against bowel cancer, say nutritionists in the Medical Research Council's Dunn Clinical Nutrition Centre in Cambridge, according to a report in *New Scientist*.

- A report from doctors at St Bartholomew's Hospital, London, suggests that slightly raised levels of cholesterol in the blood only increase the risk of heart attacks in heavy smokers, those with a family history of heart disease or those who are very overweight. But a low-fat, high natural starch diet will still keep you fitter.

- Researchers at the Reading Institute of Food Research have discovered that a low-fat, high-carbohydrate meal at breakfast produces the maximum mental alertness for the rest of the morning.

• Acid, Alkali and pH •

These are terms that have produced considerable confusion for those trying to follow the food combining lifestyle, since Dr Hay wrote his books in the 1930s. The problem has arisen because the terminology has changed.

Acids such as hydrochloric acid, nitric acid or sulphuric acid are strong acids. A molecule of hydrochloric acid consists of one negative ion of chlorine and one positive ion of hydrogen. In water, the ions separate completely and can react quickly and strongly with other ions in solution.

pH is the measure of the hydrogen ion concentration in a solution. A pH of 1 is a strong acid with many hydrogen ions. A pH of 14 has few hydrogen ions and is a strong alkali. A pH of 7 is a neutral solution.

Acids such as citric acid or ethanoic acid (vinegar) are weak acids. Although molecules of these acids still contain positive hydrogen ions, they do not separate completely in water.

Substances that can neutralize acids are called bases. If a base will also dissolve in water it is called an alkali.

Alkalis such as sodium hydroxide and potassium hydroxide are strong alkalis. A molecule of sodium hydroxide consists of one positive sodium ion and one negative hydroxide ion. In water the ions separate completely.

Alkalis such as sodium hydrogencarbonate (bicarbonate of soda) and ammonium hydroxide are weak alkalis. The hydroxide ions do not separate completely in water.

Calcium carbonate is a base. It is not soluble in water, but will react to neutralize an acid and to release carbon dioxide gas.

Blood, lymph and the fluids that bathe our cells must stay within a very narrow pH. Any tendency to change has to be counteracted straight away. The body produces substances called buffers, which react with any acid or alkali to maintain a constant pH. The most important buffer is sodium hydrogencarbonate.

The mineral ions of sodium, calcium and potassium used to be called the 'alkaline earth elements', because they form the positive ions of strong alkalis. If food containing these elements is burnt in oxygen and the ash dissolved in water, an alkali is obtained.

Dr Hay's references to alkaline foods are simply an injunction to eat foods that have useful levels of calcium and potassium salts: to eat plenty of fresh fruit and vegetables every day.

Protein in the diet which is not needed for growth or repair of tissue has to be destroyed. The amino acids are converted into urea and uric acid, which have to pass into the bloodstream to be eliminated by the kidneys. A high-protein diet results in the production of excess acid which can put the acid/alkali balance under strain, as well as causing problems for the kidney which has to eliminate the acid.

● The Main Groups of Foods: Carbohydrates, Fats and Protein ●

Carbohydrates are compounds of carbon, hydrogen and oxygen. They are the main source of energy in food.

Fats are compounds of fatty acids and glycerol, again built from carbon, hydrogen and oxygen, but with less oxygen than the carbohydrates. This makes them a more compact form of energy.

Proteins all contain nitrogen, in addition to carbon, hydrogen and oxygen. They form the tissues that make living things work and control the processes within the cells.

• Carbohydrates •

Most of our food starts off in the green leaves of plants, where the energy from sunlight is trapped. This energy is then used to join a molecule of water to a molecule of carbon dioxide to form a simple sugar. If the plant wants this energy for some other purpose it can split the simple sugar and add oxygen to the parts, to re-form water and carbon dioxide. The energy is then used to keep all the living processes in the cell going.

Unfortunately for the plant, simple sugars are not easily stored in its cells, because they dissolve in water. To overcome this problem, the plant joins two simple sugars together to make a slightly larger sugar molecule, and then joins these in long chains to make starch. These starch molecules are an excellent way of storing the sun's energy and are the main source of energy in food.

However, for some purposes starches take up too much space. The same energy can be stored in a small space if the molecules are altered to produce oils and fats. Plants will often manufacture oils to store energy for seeds and nuts.

Starches and sugars are known as carbohydrates, because they contain only the elements carbon, hydrogen and oxygen.

Starches are also known as polysaccharides – compounds built of many sugar molecules. Non-starch polysaccharides are known collectively as dietary fibre.

Sugars

Monosaccharides (single sugars), such as glucose and fructose, are the simplest sugars. The more complex sugars and starches are broken down into these during digestion.

Disaccharides (two sugars), such as sucrose, maltose and lactose, are formed of two simple sugar molecules linked together. Many people cannot digest lactose (milk sugar) as they grow older.

Sugars inside fruit, or formed by the digestion of starch, are released slowly from food and absorbed steadily by the bloodstream. Sugars added to food or drinks are digested much more quickly, and surges of sugar entering the bloodstream can cause fluctuations in blood-sugar levels that have a harmful effect on health.

Non-sugar sweeteners provide a sweet alternative to sugar, but since they are all highly processed, and not a useful part of the diet, they are best avoided.

Starch

Polysaccharides are long chains of glucose molecules, which are formed into granules in the storage organs of plants. They are insoluble in water and in this form are indigestible. When heated with water, the starch absorbs the water, swells and gelatinizes and can then be broken down by the digestive system. If the processing takes place without water, part of the starch remains indigestible. This happens in the production of some breakfast cereals.

Dietary fibre consists of the cellulose cell walls and the pectins and gums that cannot be digested by the human system (although they can be digested by a cow). Dietary fibre helps the correct passage of food through the digestive system. A diet rich in fresh fruit and vegetables will provide sufficient fibre. Excess fibre can trap minerals such as calcium, iron, copper and zinc. Wheat fibre is also abrasive and in excess can scratch the lining of the digestive system.

• Fats •

Fats are combinations of fatty acids and glycerol. A mixture of all types of fatty acids is needed for normal health.

Saturated fats

These have their carbon chain saturated with hydrogen atoms. They are stable fats and keep well. Palmitic acid and stearic acid form butter, lard, suet and cocoa butter. Myristic acid forms part of butter and coconut oil.

Unsaturated fats

If hydrogen atoms are missing from the carbon chain, the carbon atoms double-bond to each other instead. Mono-unsaturated fats have a single double-bond, but poly-unsaturated fats have more double-bonds. These double bonds are more reactive and the fat easily combines with oxygen from the air to go rancid.

Oleic acid forms 60–70 per cent of olive oil and rapeseed oil.

Linoleic acid is found in seed oils, such as maize, soya and sunflower.

Linolenic occurs in vegetable oils in small amounts.

Arachidonic acid only occurs in animal fats, but it can be formed from linoleic acid.

Decosahexaenoic acid is found in oily fish.

The double-bonds in natural unsaturated fats are normally in the 'cis' position. This is the natural structure that the body expects. When margarine is being manufactured, some of these bonds are changed into the 'trans' position. These are totally alien to our bodies. These 'trans' fats may increase levels of blood cholesterol and increase the risk of heart disease.

• Proteins •

All living things need to be able to do far more than simply store energy. Almost all living things are built from vast collections of cells, which have to be able to grow. They also move or move materials within the cells, exchange messages with other cells, and most are able to reproduce. Eventually all cells die. In order to carry out these important life processes, a cell needs many different proteins.

Proteins are large, complex molecules built from over 20 different amino acids to form long, complex chains of hundreds or thousands of amino acid units. When a plant cell is producing protein, it first uses the energy of sunlight to join nitrogenous compounds and sugar to make amino acids. Then it joins these amino acids in a very precise way, in long chains, which curl up into complicated 3D shapes. A protein has to have the right amino acids in the correct order, just as each recipe in this book is built from 26 letters of the alphabet, but they must all be in the right order if the recipe is to make sense, and work. Some of these amino acids are common in plants, but others are rare.

Humans, like most other animals, are unable to manufacture these amino acids from their elements. We have to eat them as protein in food, then break them down into their building blocks, amino acids. We cannot simply use plant protein, or other animal protein. We have to make human protein.

Amino acids are needed to produce the proteins that make the walls of human or animal cells, as well as most of the complicated structures within every cell. They are also needed to form the protein that is the part of a muscle cell that contracts, as well as the tough surface of a skin cell. Proteins also form the fine tendrils of nerve cells.

Proteins called enzymes also control all the processes that take place in every cell to keep us alive, both inside cells, and outside cells in our digestive system.

There are 20 different amino acids, but they can be arranged in an infinite number of ways. It is the sequence of amino acids in the chain, and the way that they cause the chain to twist and fold, that determines the function of the protein. In digestion, the protein chain is split into the individual amino acids. These are then reassembled in our cells to form the wide variety of human protein.

Indispensable amino acids must be obtained from the food that we eat. These are isoleucine, leucine, lysine, methionine, phenylalanine, threonine, tryptophan and valine. Histidine is also essential in the diet of young children.

The following amino acids are also essential, but they can be manufactured inside our own bodies by breaking down and re-assembling other amino acids: alanine, arginine, asparagine, aspartic acid, cysteine, glutamic acid, glutamine, glycine, proline, serine and tyrosine.

The amino acids in animal proteins from meat, fish, milk, cheese and eggs match closely those required by humans. Plant proteins often have a marked imbalance of amino acids. Wheat and rice are low in lysine, peas and beans are low in tryptophan and methionine. Mixtures of a broad variety of plant foods will produce a balance of amino acids closer to our requirements. Mixtures of cereals provide the main source of protein for many people.

Surplus protein cannot be stored in our bodies, and if energy is in short supply, protein will be broken down as an energy source rather than being used for growth.

• Vitamins, Minerals and Trace Elements •

If you follow the food combining lifestyle you will get all the vitamins, minerals and trace elements that you require without the need to take any supplements.

Vitamins

Always serve green vegetables with a dab of butter or add a dressing of olive oil, as this increases the absorption of vitamins by the body. This is because these vitamins are soluble only in oil, not water.

- Vitamin A: retinol is made inside our bodies from beta carotene, which gives the orange and yellow colour to fruits and vegetables. Good sources are carrots, sweet potatoes, apricots, mangoes, yellow-fleshed melons, peaches, nectarines, pumpkins, tomatoes, spinach, watercress and dark green leafy vegetables. We only make as much vitamin A as we need.

- Vitamin A is also found in liver, kidney, cheese, eggs and cod-liver oil. Smaller amounts are obtained from yogurt, milk, butter and oily fish, such as mackerel and sardines. If we eat too much liver, we can overdose on vitamin A and suffer from joint pains until we have used up the excess. One meal of liver per week provides a good source of iron without excess vitamin A. Pregnant women should not eat liver, as the excess vitamin A can damage the foetus.

- Vitamin A is important for the care of the eyes, and to help the immune system fight off infection. It is essential for normal growth and the repair of tissues. It is also important in reducing the risk of cancer and heart disease.

- Vitamin B_1: thiamine is needed to release the energy from food. Good sources are potatoes, wholegrain cereals, green vegetables, pulses, nuts and sunflower seeds. Diets high in refined starch can suffer from B_1 deficiency.

- Vitamine B_2: riboflavine is also needed to release the energy from food. Good sources are liver, meat, milk and cheese.

- Vitamine B_3 (PP): niacin, or nicotinic acid, is needed to release the energy from food. Good sources are peas and beans, liver, meat and wholegrain cereals. This vitamin is unavailable in maize unless treated with alkali. The body can also make niacin from the tryptophan present in eggs.

- Vitamin B_5: pantothenic acid is needed to make energy available to the body's cells. Good sources are eggs, liver, kidney, cheese, mushrooms, peanuts and bananas.

- Vitamin B_6: pyridoxine is needed to make proper use of proteins. Good sources are liver, cereal, pulses and poultry. Supplements are potentially dangerous, as an excess can result in nerve damage.

- Vitamin B_{12}: cobalamin is essential for the formation of red blood cells. Good sources are meat, milk, cheese and eggs. Vegans are at risk from a characteristic anaemia as B_{12} does not occur in vegetable food.

- Vitamin B(M): folic acid is also essential for the formation of red blood cells. Good sources are broccoli, spinach, Brussels sprouts and other green leafy vegetables, beetroot, broad beans, sweet corn, eggs, liver and wholegrain cereals. The Department of Health advises 400µg (microgrammes) a day for pregnant women to reduce the risk of spina bifida.

- Vitamin B(H): biotin is needed to make energy available from fat. Good sources are liver, kidney, pork, wholegrain cereals, lentils, nuts and cauliflower. It is also produced by bacteria in the large intestine.

- Vitamin C: ascorbic acid is essential to keep our connective tissues healthy and to heal wounds. It is also needed to enable iron to be absorbed from food. Good sources are blackcurrants, cherries, strawberries, kiwi fruit, gooseberries, peppers, guavas, oranges, sprouts, cauliflowers and potatoes. Vitamin C is water-soluble, so cook vegetables by steaming or in a microwave without adding water. Use the water that vegetables are cooked in to make soups or sauces.

- Vitamin D: calciferol helps the body to make proper use of calcium in bones and teeth. Good sources are sunlight, oily fish, eggs, butter and yogurt. Too high an intake of vitamin D can result in excess calcium being absorbed from the food, resulting in damage to the kidneys.

- Vitamin E: tocopherol mops up dangerous chemicals in the bloodstream – 100IU (international units) a day has been shown to be beneficial. Good sources are eggs, butter, vegetable oil, oily fish, almonds, avocados, pine kernels, wholegrain cereals and sunflower seeds.

- Vitamin F: linoleic and alpha linolenic acids. These are known to be essential for the correct structuring of cell membranes. Vegetable oils are a good source.

Minerals

Almost all minerals are found in the human body, and 15 of them are known to be essential. They will be absorbed in the right amounts in a properly balanced and combined diet, but most of the trace elements and iron and zinc are poisonous if extra is consumed.

- Potassium is essential to maintain the right balance of acids and alkalis in the body. It is needed in order to excrete excess acid. Low levels of potassium in the diet are linked to high blood pressure and an increased risk of strokes. Good sources are tomatoes, fruit, yogurt, cheese, potatoes, soya products, wholegrain cereals, nuts and black treacle. Deficiency is unlikely to occur on the diet described by this book unless diuretics or purgatives are taken, or in cases of diarrhoea linked to malnutrition.

- Iron is needed for the production of red blood cells, for muscle tissue and for handling oxygen in many other cells. Good sources are liver, red meat, fish, raisins and sultanas and green vegetables. Tannins from tea and an excess of wheat fibre can reduce the uptake of iron.

- Magnesium is essential for healthy bones, nerves and muscles. Good sources are nuts, raisins and sultanas, bananas and soya products. Deficiency is rare except in cases of severe diarrhoea.

- Zinc is needed for the growth of all healthy tissue, muscle and bone, and for the healing of wounds. Good sources are red meat, liver and hard cheese but zinc uptake is reduced if cereal fibre is eaten at the same time. Wholegrain cereals also contain useful levels of zinc.

- Phosphorus is an important part of all healthy cells, especially bones and teeth. Good sources are meat and other proteins.

- Calcium is needed for healthy bones and teeth. Good sources are milk and cheese, yogurt, wholegrain cereals, pulses, vegetables and raisins and sultanas. Vitamin D is essential for the correct uptake of calcium from the diet. Wheat fibre also reduces calcium uptake.

- Sodium and chloride are both essential elements for muscle and nerve activity. A diet rich in processed foods is likely to contain excessively high sodium levels and to increase the risk of high blood pressure.

Trace Elements

These are the elements that are essential for the body to work, but needed only in very small amounts.

- Chromium is needed for insulin production. Good sources are shellfish, brewers' yeast, beef, chicken, wholegrain cereals, nuts and black treacle.

- Copper is used in the manufacture of red blood cells and many enzymes. Good sources are shellfish, kidney, wholegrain cereals, liver, green vegetables, fish.

- Iodine is needed to make thyroid hormones and for the development of the nervous system. Good sources are fish, shellfish, milk and wholegrain cereals, but vegans may be prone to low iodine levels.

- Selenium is important for some enzymes. Good sources are liver, meat, fish and wholegrain cereals.

- Manganese is needed in order for many enzymes to operate. Cereals and nuts are good sources.

• Digestion: How It Works •

Our digestive system evolved over many millions of years, matching the lifestyle of our ancestors, who hunted for meat or fish and gathered seeds, fruits, roots and berries.

The change in our ancestors' way of life to an agricultural and then an industrial lifestyle was so quick that the power of evolution to match the way our body works to the way we live has not yet had time to operate. We still have a digestive system designed to match millions of years of a hunter-gatherer existence.

Animals like the cow, which evolved to eat only vegetable food, have developed a series of pouches, or extra stomachs, to separate one meal from the next. As digestion progresses, food is moved from one to the next, or even brought back to the mouth for a further chew.

Our bodies are designed to work best using a variety of different types of food. Our digestive system is designed to cope in two distinct ways, according to whether the food is mostly protein or mostly starch.

The process of making food available for our cells to use starts with cooking. Starches in cereals, pulses and tubers need to be softened and gelatinized by a period of moist cooking before they can be digested. Cellulose cell walls need to be ruptured by the cooking process before the contents are accessible to digestion. Meat fibres also need to be softened to improve their digestibility.

Cooking also destroys the toxins that many plants contain. For example, red kidney beans require overnight soaking and then boiling rapidly for 10 minutes before they are safe to eat.

Food in the mouth is broken down mechanically and mixed with salivary amylase, or enzymes. The amylase will only start the digestion of starch in a neutral solution. If the food is acid it will not work. If the starch is coated in fat, then digestion of the starch will be limited.

The stomach produces gastric juice in response to the food entering the stomach. About 5½ pints/3 litres of juice are produced each day. The strong muscular walls mix the food with the gastric juices, which contain much more of the enzyme pepsin and more hydrochloric acid when protein enters the stomach. This is a 0.2–0.4 per cent solution of acid, which is much stronger than acid foods. The acid provides the conditions needed for the digestion of protein, as well as destroying most bacteria eaten with the food. A protein meal will remain for 2–4 hours in the stomach.

A starch and vegetable meal will pass through the stomach very quickly, without stimulating the production of large amounts of acid or pepsin.

Fat can bring digestion in the stomach to a standstill. The contents remain acid for a prolonged period and this can give rise to discomfort.

Small amounts of water, minerals such as sodium chloride, most B vitamins, vitamin C and alcohol are all absorbed directly from the stomach. Simple sugars are also absorbed, and if the food contains too much sugar this can result in a dangerous surge in blood-sugar levels.

The semi-liquid partially digested food (chyme) is then allowed to move slowly into the small intestine. Here, bile from the liver emulsifies the fats into tiny droplets. An alkaline liquid from the pancreas neutralizes the stomach acid. In the neutral solution the enzyme lipase splits the fats into fatty acids and glycerol, the enzyme amylase splits starch into maltose. The enzymes trypsin and chymotripsin continue to split proteins into short-chain peptides and amino acids.

The final stages of digestion take place when the food is in contact with the cells that line the walls of the small intestine. The food molecules are absorbed by the cells and any remaining peptides are split into amino acids, maltose is converted to glucose, sucrose into glucose and fructose, lactose into glucose and galactose. Most of the absorption of digested food takes place through the surface of the small intestine, whose surface area is greatly increased by tiny finger-like projections called villi. Laxatives and excessive fibre interfere with the absorption of food here, and phytic acid in wholemeal breakfast cereals can interfere with the uptake of calcium, iron and zinc.

The remaining cellulose, and other fibre and indigestible remains, are now processed by bacteria in the large intestine. These bacteria form some B vitamins as well as useful amounts of vitamin K, which are absorbed through the walls of the large intestine.

All the products of the digestion of starch and sugars form

simple sugars, which are carried by the bloodstream directly to the liver. The liver keeps close control of the level of sugar in the blood, supplying the tissues with a constant level of glucose and storing the surplus as glycogen in the liver and muscles. When the glycogen reserves are full, further surplus sugar is converted into fat for storage.

Fatty acids absorbed by the small intestine do not pass directly into the bloodstream, but are converted back into fats and added to the lymph fluid. This rejoins the bloodstream but bypasses the liver. The fat circulates in the bloodstream and is available as an energy source for the body cells. Fat in the diet is more easily converted into body fat than carbohydrate is.

Don't mix starch meals with protein meals

A protein meal of meat, cheese or eggs is broken up by the teeth and passed down to the stomach. In response to the arrival of the protein, the stomach lining produces a strong acid and enzymes that digest protein in acid solution, and a thick, sticky mucus to protect the lining of the stomach from attack by its own enzymes. These enzymes snip the long protein molecules in our food into shorter chains and then into individual amino acids.

A meal of protein may take several hours for complete digestion before passing on into the small intestine. Here the stomach acid is neutralized by bile salts from the liver. The pancreas now adds further protein-digesting enzymes to complete the process and the soup of amino acids is absorbed through the villi that line the small intestine and passed on into the bloodstream.

A meal of starch, on the other hand, is partly digested in the mouth, where chewing mixes enzymes in the alkaline saliva with the food. The starch molecule is split into sugar molecules. A starch meal does not stimulate the stomach to produce acid or protein-digesting enzymes, and the food is passed on to the small intestine within an hour. Once there, further enzymes are added in an alkaline solution that completes the breakdown of starches into sugars. These are also absorbed through the villi that line the small intestine and pass into the bloodstream.

This system works efficiently only if starch and protein appear as separate meals. The food combining lifestyle puts this scientific knowledge into practice.

If starch is mixed with protein, then the enzymes in the stomach are diluted and the stomach feels full for longer, because the digestion of protein is inefficient. Acid is being produced for every mixed meal, which puts the stomach under stress. The acid has to be neutralized by the bile salts for every meal, which in turn puts the small intestine under stress.

Eat wholegrain cereals, not highly refined flour

Wholegrain cereals contain starch with a little protein. They are digested comparatively slowly, but efficiently, by the starch-digestion process, but there are enough protein-digesting enzymes in the small intestine to ensure that the proteins as well as the starches are digested. The sugars that result from the digestion of starch are absorbed by the villi and passed into the bloodstream for several hours. The liver is able to convert sugars not immediately required into glycogen for storage. If more sugar is absorbed than can be converted into glycogen, the surplus will be changed into fat.

White flour is almost pure starch. It mixes easily with saliva in the mouth and breaks down rapidly into sugars. As soon as the digested starch reaches the small intestine, a huge surge of sugars passes into the bloodstream. Insulin is produced rapidly to control it and the liver is put under stress to process the surplus. The body works flat out to remove the surplus from the bloodstream and usually overshoots, leaving the bloodstream with too low sugar levels and the person feeling tired and lacking in energy. These fluctuating blood-sugar levels can put the body under too much stress and the system controlling blood sugar then starts to break down. The result may be diabetes.

Refined sugar is even worse, because it requires no further digestion but enters the bloodstream in a dangerous surge.

Dr Hay was critical of potatoes in the diet because their starch is easily digested, but they are a useful source of starch and vitamin C. The skins of potatoes should always be eaten, as most vitamins and minerals lie close to the surface and are removed by peeling.

No more than one protein meal each day

Protein is digested to become amino acids, which are then absorbed into the bloodstream. These amino acids are subsequently absorbed by all cells that require them for growth or the repair of tissue and are built up again into human protein.

All amino acids not needed for growth and repair have to be destroyed. The liver removes the amino group and converts the rest into sugar and then into glycogen or fat. The amino group has to be converted into urea, which is then removed from the blood by the kidneys.

Both the amino group and urea form an acid solution. Potassium and calcium are needed to neutralize this acid and are lost to the body. Excess protein in the diet therefore puts the liver under stress. The loss of calcium may be made up by removing calcium from the bones, and the loss of potassium makes it more difficult for the body to balance the acid and alkaline substances in solution. The kidney has to deal with the acid end-product of excess protein in the diet and is also put under stress.

One protein meal a day provides most of us with all the protein that we need.

• Evolution, Diet and Appetite •

Our ancestors for many millions of years ate a diet based on starchy foods, fruit and vegetables, with the occasional meal of protein to provide for growth and repair of tissue. They were rarely exposed to fat that wasn't closely linked to the plant or animal from which it came. As a result, our appetite mechanisms evolved to work on starch meals or on protein meals to ensure the delicate balance between the food we need and the food we eat. To this day our digestive systems work most efficiently when protein and starch meals are kept separate. There have been too few generations of humans since our diets changed for our digestive systems to cope well with the food mixtures that are now available.

❦ CHAPTER 3 ❦
Food Combining and Maintaining Health

● Don't Forget Your Doctor ●

Recent research has shown that a lot of ill health is diet-related, and avoidable, but this does not mean that all health can be cured by a change of diet.

There are many infectious and contagious diseases that can only be prevented by vaccination, and the risk to health from vaccination is far smaller than the potential risk from not being vaccinated and catching the disease.

There are many other conditions where it is only the skilled diagnosis of a qualified medical doctor and the proper pre-scribed treatment that can effect a cure.

If you think you are ill you should consult a doctor. This book is not a substitute for the doctor's medical experience.

● General Health Tips ●

Eat some foods high in potassium and calcium every day

The chemical reactions inside all our cells are very sensitive to the balance of acid and alkali. This balance is maintained by ions of calcium, potassium, sodium, chloride, phosphate and hydrogencarbonate.

If we eat excess protein or acid foods, calcium and potassium ions get used up in order to neutralize the acid. Dr Hay and modern scientists advocate the same two approaches. Don't eat too much protein and do eat high potassium foods every day. Dr Hay also advocates restricting the intake of acid foods, such as rhubarb and vinegar, but modern food chemistry demonstrates that a touch of vinegar in cooking a protein meal will help preserve many of the vitamins, such as thiamin, riboflavin, folate and vitamin C.

Eat starch according to your needs

Women require only one starch meal each day, unless they are active and need the extra energy. Men need extra energy and may require two starch meals a day.

On average, women have a more efficient metabolism than men. If you have a very low-fat diet, you will need to eat more starch than you can comfortably eat in one sitting. If you have a physically active life, two starch meals a day may give you all the energy you need.

Eat plenty of non-starchy vegetables – as much as you like!

Non-starchy vegetables may not provide you with vast amounts of energy, but they do provide important essential vitamins, minerals and trace elements. Eat a wide variety and use them to fill up your plate at any meal. Use fresh or frozen vegetables and cook by steaming or microwaving for the best nutritional value.

Eat a wide variety of fruit and vegetables

There is no one food that has all the ingredients you need. If you eat a wide variety, you ensure that you get sufficient of all the vitamins and minerals that your body requires. There is some evidence that eating a little of a lot of different foods greatly reduces the chance of developing food allergies. This applies particularly to the main starch foods, so don't eat wheat and potatoes all the time.

Which Way to Health recommends that you eat as much as you like of fruit and vegetables. Your target should be five portions a day. These foods are full of vitamins and fibre, but low in calories. Don't worry too much about pesticides in or on fruit: for most of us, heart disease is a much bigger risk. If you are worried, buy organic fruit and vegetables or grow your own.

In the UK the highest incidence of heart disease occurs in people who eat the least fruit and vegetables. The more fruit and vegetables you eat, the less likely you are to develop cancer of the lung, stomach, mouth, cervix, colon or rectum.

Eat plenty of fresh fruit – as much as you like!

Fresh fruit contains far more vitamins than cooked fruit. It makes an ideal snack between meals and is superb for that 'feel-good' factor.

Some fruits, like bananas, dates and plantains, are starchy. Others, like citrus fruit, are acid. Most can be eaten with any protein meal.

Use olive oil if you need oil for cooking or dressings

Olive oil is an easily digested, mono-unsaturated oil and is a good source of vitamin E. Extra-virgin cold-pressed oil is best. It is the basic oil of the healthy Mediterranean lifestyle. Cretans, in particular, have the second lowest rate of heart disease in the world.

You can eat butter and cream in moderation

Butter or margarine? Should you eat saturated fats or poly-unsaturated fats? Margarines are highly processed and refined foods. If you keep your fat intake low, you can allow yourself butter and cream (1 oz/25 g of each per day). Both of these are pure, natural foods. Butter is an excellent source of vitamin E and is pure dairy fat. Single cream is 20 per cent fat and is a good source of vitamins A, E and D.

A certain amount of fat is essential in our diet. Provided that your overall intake of fat is kept low, butter and cream will enhance your lifestyle and help you maintain your health.

Don't smother starch meals in fat

A healthy starch meal can easily be overloaded with an unhealthy fatty sauce. A baked potato with a small lump of butter, or potato chips dipped in olive oil and drained before roasting in the oven make excellent meals, but if the potato is soaked in fat you will suffer all the risks of a high-fat diet.

Don't add sugar

Sugar is absorbed too quickly into the bloodstream. It results in swings in blood-sugar level that put a strain on all the regulation systems in the body. High blood-sugar levels can increase damage in all the tissues that the blood bathes.

Sugar adds nothing useful to the diet. You get a much more useful supply of energy from eating starchy foods.

Black treacle, molasses and honey contain useful minerals and vitamins. Use these in moderation.

Don't add extra salt

Salt, or sodium chloride, is essential in very small amounts in our diet, but it is easy to eat far too much. The surplus salt has to be excreted by the kidneys. This makes them work harder and increases the risk of kidney failure.

Salt can also prevent the uptake of calcium and lead to poor bone development in children.

A little cholesterol is essential for health

Cholesterol is an essential compound, most of which is manufactured in our livers and circulated throughout our bodies. High-cholesterol foods such as shellfish and eggs are now thought to have little effect on blood cholesterol levels. Low cholesterol levels can result in severe depression.

You can slash your risk of heart disease by eating two portions of oily fish, such as herring or mackerel, each week. Blood pressure and inflammation can be reduced and controlled by eating fish oils that contain omega-3 fatty acids. The best sources of these are mackerel, sardines, salmon, pilchards and herring. But note: you can overdose on fish oil supplements – vitamins A and D are toxic in high amounts.

Low-fat diets also reduce your risk of skin cancer, according to dermatologists in Houston, Texas.

Don't eat excessive amounts of bran

Eating excessive amounts of bran can prevent your body from absorbing essential calcium, iron, zinc and copper. Wheat fibre can be rough and irritating to the human digestive system. If you eat wholegrain cereals and plenty of fresh fruit and vegetables, you don't need to add extra fibre to your diet.

Additional tips

- A *New Scientist* report states that: 'New research from Britain and the US, as well as Japan, provides strong evidence that women can substantially reduce the risk of breast cancer by consuming soya bean products, such as soya milk, or tofu.'

- The *New Scientist* report also states that 'Researchers in Cambridge have shown that a diet high in soya protein can alter women's hormones in a way that mimics the anti-cancer drug Tamoxifen.' 'Eating soya products can lower the risk of both prostate and colon cancers.' 'Most natural high-fibre foods, such as wholewheat, oats, barley, rye, sesame and flax seeds, may have a similar effect.'

- Borage seed oil (starflower oil) is high in gamma linolenic acid. Its anti-inflammatory properties help reduce swelling and tenderness of joints in rheumatoid arthritis. It has higher levels of this acid than evening primrose oil.

- Cranberry juice can help protect against all types of urinary infection according to researchers in Boston, USA.

- Garlic has strong antibiotic properties.

- Don't go on a calorie-reduced diet to slim without taking plenty of exercise. Without the exercise you lose muscle, not fat. You'll simply end up weak and fat!

- Red wine in moderation is good for older people only. A lot of red wine damages your liver. For younger people the risks of developing liver cancer outweigh the health benefits of a glass of wine.

- If you suffer from mouth ulcers you may be short of B vitamins, particularly thiamine, riboflavin and B_6.

- Women who suffer from prolonged or heavy periods are likely to develop an iron deficiency.

- Women who have premenstrual syndrome may lack vitamins B and C.

- Vegetarians may develop iron deficiency.

- Convenience foods are often low in vitamin B and magnesium.

- If you don't eat fresh fruit and vegetables every day you may lack vitamin C, magnesium and potassium.

- Heavy smokers need a much higher intake of vitamin C for good health.

- Older people need to increase their intake of vitamin B, calcium, potassium and iron.

- If you are tired all the time researchers at Addenbrooke's Hospital in Cambridge think low levels of folic acid may be part of the cause.

• Health is Also Dependent on Exercise •

It does not matter what age you are. You need exercise to stay fit and healthy.

You are aiming at a minimum of three sessions of 30 minutes' vigorous exercise each week. A better target is a 30-minute session every day. If you try to do too much too quickly you risk damage to joints and muscles and will end up stiff and sore.

If you are not fit now, you must start slowly and build yourself up. Time yourself with an alarm clock. Start with just one minute of exercise on the first day, two minutes on the second day, three minutes on the third. Continue adding just one minute to the exercise period each day, until at the end of 30 days you will have painlessly achieved your target – which you must now maintain every day!

It is best to select several different types of exercise that you really enjoy and can keep doing. The exercise should leave you feeling good, looking forward to the next session and should develop stamina, strength and suppleness. Swimming hard is one of the few exercises that develops all three qualities at the same time.

Vigorous exercise should leave you puffed, hot and sweaty! But if you feel muscle pain, stop. If you feel dizzy, or break out in a cold sweat, or suffer pains in the chest, neck or upper left arm, stop, and if it happens again then consult your doctor.

If you are very unfit it may be wise to check with a doctor before you start a new exercise programme, particularly if you are over 60. You should also check with your doctor if you have high blood pressure, heart disease, joint pains or diabetes.

It is not wise to exercise strongly within two hours of a meal, within one hour of drinking alcohol, or in very hot or very cold conditions. But gentle exercise helps digestion – the muscles of the abdomen gently massage the digestive system, encouraging it to mix and move the digesting food. Tight belts or corsets can restrict the digestive system and produce symptoms of indigestion.

• Stress, Relaxation and Sleep •

Stress in excess is the cause of a wide range of disorders, both mental and physical. The food combining diet seems to make us more resilient to excess stress, but we need to be aware of the symptoms and take control of our own lives. Stress can result from any situation where we feel we are not confident or in control. Such situations cannot always be avoided, but we can take steps to reduce the level of stress that we experience.

Stress can result in difficulty in sleeping, or in sleeping too much, when we don't want to wake up and face the world. It can cause appetite problems, indigestion and stomach upsets, diarrhoea and frequent urination. It can produce headaches, muscle tension, clenched jaws and grinding teeth. It can result in nervousness, mood swings, irritability and angry outbursts.

Identifying the sources of stress and recognizing how they are affecting you is the first step in keeping stress under control. If possible, stop for a few minutes and take several slow, deep breaths before continuing whatever you are doing, and ensure you get a good night's sleep.

- Eat a light starch meal early in the evening.

- Avoid drinking tea, coffee or alcohol after mid-afternoon.

- Ensure you have enough exercise every day.

- Check that your bed is comfortable and your bedroom at a reasonable temperature.

- Don't watch exciting television or video programmes – or the news – last thing at night.

- Keep a pad and pen by the bed and jot down any ideas you want to remember; don't try to solve your problems last thing at night.

• Avoiding Pollution •

The biggest pollutants of food can be in the home itself.

The greatest risk, particularly to children, comes from old medicines and household and garden chemicals. Remove all old and unmarked tins, jars and bottles and take them to your local waste point for safe disposal. Don't reuse old containers for food. Only food-grade plastic or glass containers should be used. Other grades may leach toxic substances into the food. Antique crocks may look fine but they can leach lead or other heavy metals from the glaze.

Make sure that all lead pipe has been removed from your water supply, particularly where old pipes join the house to the main supply. A water-filter jug can improve the quality of drinking water as well as the taste.

Don't eat produce grown beside a busy road. This can accumulate lead and other toxic compounds from the remains of fuel, rubber and brake linings.

Take extreme care when applying pesticides to home-grown produce. It is very difficult to get uniform coverage at the absolute minimum level needed to kill just the pests. The danger from pesticides on produce purchased from a supermarket is tiny by comparison.

• Avoiding Pesticides on Food •

A caterpillar on your cauliflower is a sign that both are safe to eat! Wash all fruit and vegetables well and discard the outer layers, where these may accumulate pesticides. The only way of being sure that your vegetables are free of pesticides is to grow them yourself, but you will then discover how hard it is to produce the unblemished, pest-free produce found on the supermarket shelves without the aid of pesticides.

Many pesticides are nerve poisons and can accumulate to dangerous levels in the body over the years. But for many people in the world the choice is to accept a low-pesticide residue on their food or starve to death, as a host of pests decimates the world's crops while they grow or destroys crops while in storage.

• Aluminium •

Aluminium in the diet is best kept as low as possible because of potential harm to the brain and the nervous system. Aluminium pots and pans are safe to use, *provided they are not cleaned until shiny*! Aluminium protects itself with a hard layer of dull grey oxide, which will prevent any aluminium from dissolving in the food. Provided this layer is left intact, aluminium is safe to use. Always wash aluminium with a soft cloth and detergent. Never scour it clean. Any food that leaves the pan bright and shiny – such as rhubarb or vinegar – should *not* be cooked in aluminium pans.

• How Cooking Affects Nutrients •

Cooking food may destroy enzymes and the chemicals that plants produce in order to try to prevent them from being palatable to animals. This may improve the flavour, texture and digestibility of the raw food.

Cooking foods in liquid and then throwing away that liquid is very wasteful of many nutrients, particularly the water-soluble vitamins, such as thiamin, riboflavin, niacin and vitamin C. There is almost never any need to discard cooking water if the right amount is used in the first place. Any surplus liquid should be used for soups and gravies, or even, as in China, served as a cold drink.

Most nutrients are lost at high temperatures and by prolonged cooking. Foods left to stand may also lose nutrients.

Microwave and infra-red cooking can improve the nutritional status of food by reducing the use of liquids and cooking times. They are good ways of reheating food, provided the food is heated right through.

Cooking protein and starches together results in destruction of the amino acid lysine, severely degrading the quality of the protein. Prolonged cooking of protein can also make it more difficult to digest.

• How Preserving Affects Nutrients •

Freezing is the best method of storing food, although the blanching of food can reduce the thiamin and vitamin C content – but this is smaller than the loss that takes place in vegetables in a box during transport to and from a shop.

Frozen foods should be kept below 0°F, −18°C, until required for use.

Food that is processed for storage in tins, cans or glass jars loses nutrients such as thiamin, folate and vitamin C as a result of the heat treatment. Other nutrients may be lost if a glass jar of food is stored in daylight.

Sulphur dioxide, which is used as a preservative, completely destroys all thiamin but helps to preserve vitamin C.

Prolonged drying in bright sunshine also destroys many of the vitamins in food. Dried foods should be stored in sealed containers to exclude both oxygen and light.

• Drinking Water •

Water is the best liquid for drinking at any age. Even infants may need some water, especially in hot weather. Children should always be allowed to drink as much water as they want (this does not apply to soft drinks, etc.). Water does not flush any nutrients out of the body, but helps to keep the kidneys working efficiently. If you are concerned about the quality of your tap water, use an ultraviolet unit to destroy any bacteria in the water and a jug filter to remove any traces of heavy metals, or boil the water before use.

• The Right Bacteria •

A healthy digestive system is populated by a wide range of bacteria, which work with our digestive systems to break down food and improve the way we absorb some vitamins. These useful bacteria help prevent disease-causing bacteria from colonizing the digestive system and making us ill. If our useful bacteria have been destroyed by a treatment with antibiotics, they need to be replaced as quickly as possible. Eating plain natural yogurt helps speed up this process.

• Fibre and Constipation •

The muscles of the walls of the small and large intestines push and pinch the digesting food, mixing it with enzymes, bringing it into close contact with the villi, which absorb the nutrients, and ensuring that the undigested food remains pass easily through the system. These muscles require something to push against. If the food is always soft or semi-liquid, the muscles lose their strength, pockets and bulges form in the intestine walls where debris accumulates, and waste becomes difficult to eliminate.

Fibre gives bulk to the food in the system and ensures that these muscles maintain their strength and can control the movement of food. The fibre also ensures that no pockets of debris are left behind and that the whole digestive system operates efficiently and is self-cleansing.

The most useful fibre comes from several portions a day of fresh fruit and vegetables, and from wholegrain cereals. Added fibre is not nearly as useful and wheat fibre is not a beneficial addition to the diet. It is too abrasive and can obstruct the absorption of minerals.

Small children should not be fed on high-fibre foods other than fresh fruit and vegetables.

• Tooth Decay •

The food combining diet can dramatically reduce tooth decay. By using wholegrains in starch meals and avoiding free sugars in drinks, sweets, cakes, biscuits and spreads, all major sources of decay are removed from the diet.

Development of a thick tooth enamel depends on the tooth biting firmly on hard food, such as chewy wholegrain and raw vegetables.

Tips for clean teeth:

• Clean between all teeth with dental floss once each day,

using a gentle up-and-down movement rather than a sawing motion.

- Pay as much attention to the back of the teeth as to the front when brushing after the last meal each day.

• Foods to Avoid •

Dr Hay was concerned about the acid from fruit and vinegar. Rhubarb and cooked tomato were also reputed to be excessively acid.

Modern methods of food analysis and a much greater understanding of the process of digestion and absorption of food can, however, help to clarify the position.

Fruit acids should not be a problem. Fresh acid fruit are an essential part of a balanced and healthy diet. They should be eaten on their own or as part of a protein meal.

Vinegar is a weak solution of ethanoic acid and this is metabolized to carbon dioxide and water. The carbon dioxide is eliminated with exhaled air and places less of a burden on the digestive system than alcohol. Vinegar should be eaten with protein rather than with starch, as it will prevent the action of the starch enzymes in the mouth. The slight acidity will also preserve the vitamins in a protein meal. Lemon juice can be used in place of vinegar in most recipes.

Similarly, cooked tomato should not be a problem as part of a protein meal, and it will also help to preserve the vitamin content of the meal.

Rhubarb contains oxalic acid. In early spring, when the amount of oxalate in the stem is low, rhubarb can safely be eaten, but by the end of May the concentration is starting to rise and rhubarb should be avoided. The oxalic acid also prevents the absorption of calcium from food and so it should not be consumed on a regular basis. The leaves of rhubarb should never be eaten.

Far more dangerous are foods made from mixtures of fat and sugar

Fat and sugar mixtures, such as biscuits and cakes, are a double danger to our bodies. Because the ingredients are highly refined, we don't know when we have eaten enough. The refined fats are absorbed quickly into the bloodstream, where they coat and clog blood vessels and have to be stored quickly in fatty tissue. The sugar has equally serious effects on the body's mechanisms. Almost all medical opinions and government health guidelines now agree that sugar and fat mixtures make a major contribution to heart disease and cancer. Avoid them!

Chocolate is also a fat/sugar mixture, which includes traces of drugs that can cause cravings and addiction. The amount of chocolate in the diet should be severely restricted.

• Food Supplements •

There is no evidence that any food supplement can produce better health than the food combining diet based on a wide range of natural ingredients. If you are following the food combining diet and are deficient in any area, then check the minerals and vitamins list for foods that are particularly high in that nutrient. If you do need supplements, you should only be taking them under proper medical supervision.

Many food supplements are dangerous if the recommended dose is exceeded, and are particularly dangerous for small children.

🍎 CHAPTER 4 🍎
Getting Started

• Changing Your Diet •

Food combining is designed to improve your quality of life. It is not a penance that you should endure. It will keep you alert and fit, and following it should not make you anxious and worried.

Any move towards the food combining lifestyle will help you improve your health and fitness. It is not an all-or-nothing diet, and it doesn't have to be adopted in full, all at once.

It's actually better if you *don't* change too quickly! The digestive system needs time to adapt to its new improved regime and to new foods. So start by reducing your consumption of sugar/fat mixtures, such as biscuits, cakes and pastry, and replace them with fresh fruit.

Try not to eat until you are hungry, don't simply eat out of habit, and don't eat everything just because it is offered to you. Drink whenever you are thirsty. Clean water is always the best way to quench a thirst.

The next step is to reduce your intake of concentrated protein – meat, fish, cheese, beans – to just one meal a day.

Slowly increase the amount of exercise that you take. It need only be by a couple of minutes each day (see pages 34–5).

• Principles of Menu Planning •

Food combining is the easy way to plan an interesting, varied and healthy diet. You don't need to count calories or measure portions. You will soon discover how much you want to eat.

Choose as wide a range of ingredients as is easily available and you will almost certainly get a balanced diet. Fill up with the starchy items for breakfast and lunch, and with the vegetables and fruit for your main meal.

• Sample Menus for a Fortnight •

Sunday

breakfast	oatmeal porridge
lunch	potato roast, fresh fruit salad
main meal	roast chicken with a selection of root and leaf vegetables (not potatoes), lemon cream

Monday

breakfast	muesli
lunch	hot garlic potatoes and salad, banana
main meal	cheese pudding with a selection of vegetables

Tuesday

breakfast	cornflakes with yogurt and sultanas
lunch	bread, butter and salad
main meal	poached fish with a selection of vegetables (not potatoes), apple pudding

Wednesday

breakfast	millet and date porridge
lunch	pasta with a pesto sauce
main meal	cottage pie, fresh fruit

Thursday

breakfast	polenta
lunch	cashew nut pilaf, fresh fruit
main meal	turkey moussaka with a selection of vegetables (not potatoes), dried fruit salad

Friday

breakfast	toast and marmalade
lunch	rice salad, fresh fruit
main meal	baked mackerel with a selection of vegetables (not potatoes), cheeses

Saturday

breakfast	rice and sultanas
lunch	baked potato and salad
main meal	citrus and almond turkey with a selection of vegetables (not potatoes), lemon cream, cheeses

Sunday

breakfast	yogurt and fresh fruit
lunch	cauliflower and potato soup, fresh fruit salad
main meal	roast ham with a selection of root and leaf vegetables (not potatoes), apple pudding

Monday

breakfast	muesli
lunch	pasta with pesto salad, dried fruit salad
main meal	sausages with a selection of vegetables

Tuesday

breakfast	cornflakes with banana
lunch	wholemeal pizza and salad
main meal	blue cheese and walnut sauce with a selection of vegetables (not potatoes), fresh fruit

Wednesday

breakfast	mixed grain bread, toasted
lunch	Persian-style rice
main meal	casserole of hearts, Greek salad, fresh fruit

Thursday

breakfast	muesli
lunch	naan bread, fresh fruit
main meal	mutton or beef stew

Friday

breakfast	toast and marmalade
lunch	rice salad, fresh fruit
main meal	grilled herring with a selection of vegetables (not potatoes), fresh fruit

Saturday

breakfast	pancakes
lunch	baked sweet potato
main meal	roast chicken with a selection of vegetables (not potatoes), cheeses, fresh fruit

• Equipment •

Pressure Cookers

The speed and efficiency of the microwave oven have caused many people to leave their pressure cookers unused at the back of a cupboard. But there is still a place for this useful item in every kitchen, and there are many dishes that are best and quickest cooked in this way. Not only does the pressure cooker save fuel by cooking so quickly (one-third of the time is a good general rule), but it also blends the flavours and tenderizes meat in a way that the average microwave cannot match.

A pressure cooker is a large saucepan with a lid, which is usually very deep. (I would always buy the one with the deep lid rather than the shallow, as you can then pile up such foods as Christmas puddings and cook two or three at once, making a further saving on fuel.) The lid is sealed with a rubber gasket and there is a control vent in the top, with a safety plug.

The cooker is designed to make use of the steam given off by foods as they cook, or by the water in which they are cooked, by confining it so that there is a rise in pressure inside the cooker and a corresponding rise in temperature. The combination of increased pressure and higher temperature forces steam through the food and reduces the cooking time.

The pressure is controlled by small weights, which are fitted on the lid – high pressure (15 lb) is suitable for general cooking purposes; medium (10 lb) is used for pre-cooking fruits for jam; low (5 lb) is best for cooking steamed puddings. Christmas puddings are especially good cooked in a pressure cooker. The appropriate pressure is always indicated in recipes. Timing starts from when the cooker reaches pressure after the weight is placed on the lid.

Pressure cookers are easy to use, but care must be taken when opening them after the cooking is finished. The cooker must always be cooled, either by allowing it to cool gradually off the heat or by holding it under cold running water, and the weight must not be removed until the cooker has stopped hissing. (My mother did this once when cooking beetroot, with the result that the newly painted kitchen ceiling and walls were suddenly splattered with purple. More importantly, she could have been badly scalded.) Always follow the manufacturer's instructions.

The pressure cooker also has a trivet, which is used inside the cooker to keep foods out of the liquid that is necessary to produce steam. Vegetables, for instance, are not cooked in water but in steam, and only a small amount of water is needed. Other foods, like steamed puddings, might burn if allowed contact with the bottom of the cooker, so they too can be stood on the trivet.

Some pressure cookers have baskets or separators, which can be fitted inside the cooker in order to cook several different foods at once. For instance, turnips may be laid on the trivet and the separators rested on top, two containing different vegetables and one containing meat.

If you live over 2,000 feet/1,600 metres above sea-level, the cooking must be calculated differently. Again, follow the manufacturer's instructions, but in most cases the time will not be increased by more than one minute for every 1,000 feet/ 1,300 metres and it may be recommended that you simply use a different weight.

Average times for foods cooked in the pressure cooker:

- Potatoes – 6 minutes

- Carrots – 6 minutes

- Meat stew – 20 minutes

- Braised, stuffed sheeps' hearts – 30 minutes

- Fish – 4 minutes

- Christmas pudding – 2lb/900g pudding at 30 minutes, steaming (without the weights) and 3 hours at 15 lb pressure. If you have a cooker with a high lid, you can cook two puddings together at the same time.

- Soups are wonderful made in the pressure cooker. In our house a chicken is never allowed to leave the house until every atom of goodness has been extracted by boiling it up in the pressure cooker. Bacon knuckles also produce a very good soup, with vegetables and lentils. The vegetables can be fresh or leftover, and quantities can be varied according to taste or what you have.

Slow Cookers

Slow cookers are designed to cook at 92°C (198°F). They should reach this temperature on a high setting within 30 minutes, or longer on a slow setting.

Slow cookers can improve the eating qualities of tough joints of meat, but they are not suitable for beans, as the temperature is too low to destroy their toxins.

Food should never be left to keep warm in the slow cooker. It should either be served hot, or cooled and refrigerated. Some slow cookers have caused problems because they don't reach a high enough temperature.

Woks

These are ideal for heat-sealing and fast cooking. Food should always be kept on the move to prevent overcooking.

Microwaves

These work well for small quantities of moist food. For larger quantities they have no advantage over conventional cooking methods. Vegetables cooked in the microwave can retain higher levels of vitamins than boiled vegetables. Large items of foods can retain cold spots in the microwave and need to stand until the heat has been conducted evenly throughout. A microwave oven temperature probe (not a glass thermometer) can be used to check that the temperature is high enough in the thickest part of the food.

Steamers

Vegetables are always best cooked in steam until tender. Boiling in water washes out many valuable nutrients.

The simplest utensil is a perforated trivet to hold the vegetables out of the boiling water in a pan, but there are many purpose-built steamers available.

Food Mixers, Food Processers, Grain Mills

Cooking your own food from the basic ingredients gives you the closest control over what you and your family eat. It allows you to stick most closely to the food combining diet and permits you to avoid all those additives that are needed to make processed foods palatable.

Fresh meat, vegetables and fruit do not need any elaborate processing. Neither do starchy meals based on rice, potatoes and vegetables. Wheat wholemeal bread from the supermarket is of high quality and can form the basis for up to half your starch meals.

The food combining diet does not include pastry, or cakes and biscuits, and so removes the need for a lot of elaborate processing equipment. A food mixer or processor is valuable if you plan to bake your own bread, and a grain mill is very useful for non-wheat flours for special diets.

• Where to Shop •

Food is freshest, and of the highest quality, in the large supermarkets. No one else can compete with their quality control and with the speed of movement from farm to shelf. They also have the highest turnover, so food ingredients have rarely been on the shelf long, and only a very few ever reach their 'best before' dates.

More unusual items can often be obtained at ethnic supermarkets and health food shops.

• Helpful Hints for the Shopper •

Fresh and frozen meat, fish, fruit and vegetables have the highest food values and the fewest additives. Buy them in quantities that you can use quickly and store them at the correct temperature. Most should be kept cool and dry.

When you look at tinned foods, select those with the fewest added ingredients. There are hundreds of additives designed to modify the texture, appearance and taste of food, which do nothing for the food value but whose health risks are as yet unknown. There is no need to avoid them altogether, but it might be wise to restrict their use as far as possible.

Many tinned foods have high salt and/or sugar levels and these are best avoided. Breakfast cereals may also contain excessive levels of salt and sugar.

• Cooking on a Budget •

If you are providing meals on a low budget, remember the cost of wasted food as well as the cost of cooking. Buy food with as little wastage as possible and trim it as little as necessary. Broad beans in their pods are mostly waste , but a solid cabbage is almost all good food. If you don't eat the fat, avoid the cheapest cuts of meat like belly pork, where you get little meat for your money, and examine the ends of your joints to select one without any thick fat layers. Always take the trouble to store food in the optimum conditions and use the most perishable foods first. Don't buy more than you need, but shopping every day can take up a lot of time, so keep a balance.

Small amounts of ready-made meals and packaged foods can cost substantially more than fresh fruit and vegetables, and the cost of meat can far outweigh its value in the diet. If you have the time, then you don't need these ready-made meals, and in many cases they take as long to prepare as fresh food.

Low-cost meals need not be monotonous, with the wide range of dried herbs and spices available in supermarkets. You use so little of these that you can afford to include them in the lowest budget meals.

If times are really hard, then eat potatoes cooked in their skins, brown rice, sprouted beans and seeds, and a little olive oil, together with herbs from your windowsill and spices. The cheapest vegetables, like carrots and cabbage, are also the healthiest and require the minimum of cooking. Fresh wholemeal bread also remains excellent value for money.

• Cooking for One •

Set yourself a target of preparing two new meals each week. It is so easy to fall back into a monotonous diet if you have only yourself to feed. Almost all starch and protein meals can be cooked following the quantities for four people, with the remainder frozen as single portions for later use. Do make sure that all containers are very clearly labelled and dated.

Fresh vegetables are easily prepared in small quantities, and you need only take the amount you need from packets of frozen vegetables. These offer high-quality food at very reasonable prices.

Give yourself time to sit and enjoy your meal, and treat it as a period for relaxation.

• Cooking for Two •

Supermarket packs often seem slightly larger than two people require, but again packs of frozen vegetables allow you to select the quantity you need and provide a much greater variety for any meal.

If two people can share the shopping and the food preparation, it can turn a routine chore into valuable time together.

• Cooking for the Family •

Our family and friends always sit down to a food combining meal, but often they do not realize that we have separated the starch from the protein. The secret is a good variety of fruit and vegetables, and a selection of sauces to accompany them.

I am a firm believer in the family sitting down for a meal together. It is part of the cement that forms a family and holds it together. It gives everyone a sense of belonging, security and identity. There should be enough variety in a meal so that the genuine likes and dislikes of family members can be tolerated, but no one should demand a meal of their own.

At a starch meal there is always a surplus of breads, rice or potatoes for anyone who is really hungry, and at protein meals we ensure there is a surplus of vegetables. We don't allow younger members of the family to raid the food cupboard if they take a dislike to what has been served. If they don't like a meal they will stay hungry until the next.

The pressure of constant advertising of unhealthy foods can

be difficult to resist, but we find that our children find much of these foods too sweet or too salt and prefer our own cooking.

We make great use of the pressure cooker to create stocks and soups and to reduce the time that we spend in the kitchen. But if a meal is needed and we are short of time, it will be bread and salad and a bowl of fruit.

Make sure that your kitchen is a safe environment for the family and start them helping to prepare family meals as soon as they are old enough to stand.

• Packed Meals •

Base all packed meals on starch. Sandwiches, salads and fresh fruit make excellent packed meals for all ages. Dried fruit and nuts add to the variety. Always ensure there is water to drink.

(Protein packed meals are more difficult to prepare and need to be kept refrigerated.)

• Ready Meals, Take-aways and Cook/Chill •

No 'modern' take-aways or cook/chill meals can match the ease of preparation, or the nutritional value, of bread, salads and an olive oil dressing. It is often cheaper to call in at the nearest supermarket for fresh fruit and vegetables for salads than to buy them ready-prepared. And a pressure cooker will often cook a protein meal, prepared from fresh ingredients, faster than it takes to thaw a frozen meal.

Where you do need ready-prepared meals, it is often easier to select a starch-based meal. But beware of excessive fat in sauces and fillings – select a low-fat and low-sugar meal. Vegetarian options often permit you to keep most closely to the food combining diet.

Food combining is the true modern lifestyle, based on a real knowledge of what is healthy and valuable in our lives, but always remember that it is not a straitjacket. It is the balance of the diet over weeks, months and years that determines your overall health.

• Drinks •

Pure water is always the best option, but for the adult a glass of wine, cider or beer with a meal will provide a pleasant alternative. Fruit juices always provide an acceptable alternative, but this is definitely second best to eating the fruit itself.

Any edible fruit can be used as a source of juice, and if prepared at home should be drunk on the day it is prepared. Cartons of fruit juices from the supermarket are a low-cost and healthy alternative.

Milk and milk shakes prepared from whole milk are always acceptable for children or adults.

For advice on drinking coffee and tea see page 82.

❦ CHAPTER 5 ❦
Entertaining and Special Occasions

• Dinner Parties •

A protein meal often produces the most attractive theme for a dinner party. Most guests will enjoy a protein meal, without realizing the lack of starch, but will lift their eyebrows if there is no protein present. Three courses are ample for any occasion.

It is often pleasant to be able to offer a choice of starter to guests. Prepare enough to offer to each guest a choice, with the host getting whatever is left.

• Entertaining on a Budget •

Meat and cheese are often the most expensive items in a meal. If you entertain on a budget, avoid these two groups of ingredients, and go instead for a range of fresh fruit and vegetables, prepared and served with sauces and spices. You are not providing your visitors with sustenance to last them a week, but with a delightful combination of flavours, colours and textures. If you feel that they will need a 'solid' meal, provide a range of fresh breads or bread rolls, together with a variety of salads and dressings.

• Eating in Restaurants •

There is nothing wrong in asking for what you want! We decide in advance whether a meal out is to be a protein or a starch meal – if you want to keep the price down, or make your choice easier, go for the starch meal. You can ask for fresh fruit or vegetable dishes without any thickened sauces with either protein or starch meals.

If you select a protein meal, avoid battered fish, pies and pizzas. Plain fish is often the easiest as it is usually served with an unthickened sauce. Roasted and grilled meats can be requested without the potatoes or rice that usually accompany them, and I always ask for extra vegetables instead. Fruit and cheese can round off a restaurant protein meal.

Starch meals can again start with fruit, or with garlic bread. If there is a selection of vegetables, I order these without a main course, together with potatoes or rice. I find the tastiest end to the meal is, again, often fresh fruit.

• Large-Scale Entertaining •

If the meal has to rest in a warm place for any length of time, it is essential to go for a starch meal. Otherwise, base it on the ideas for the dinner party above.

Quantities are always difficult, but you can ensure a plentiful supply of potatoes, bread or rice for a starch meal. Generally people eat far less than you expect (unless they are teenagers or students home from college, when they eat far more than anyone would dream possible). People moving round with a glass of wine in their hands and a small plate will eat less than if they sit down at a table.

When cooking larger quantities of any food, it will take far longer than you expect to get large pans up to cooking temperature. You should ensure that the food is well mixed so that it is evenly heated.

Domestic microwaves are suitable only for small quantities of food.

• Picnics and Children's Party Ideas •

Starch-based meals are easiest to prepare in advance. Almost any recipe could be used – it depends on what the children prefer!

The simplest ideas are often the best.

- Bread or rolls and butter
- Wide range of salad (see pages 230–4) and crudités (see page 244)
- Starch (see pages 152–4) or oil sauces and dips (see pages 210–21)
- Wide range of fresh fruit (see pages 75–6)
- Dairy ice cream

• Barbecues •

The Australian-style barbie, which uses a thick, solid steel plate over the flames, is much easier to use than the wire-mesh grills through which the flames burn the meat.

A plentiful supply of meat plus protein sauces and dips can be accompanied by vegetable kebabs. If you are preparing a barbecue for a large number, meat can be pre-cooked in a conventional oven and then quickly seared over the flame before serving.

• Christmas •

If you want to forget food combining over Christmas, go ahead, but you may find that you prefer to keep to your diet.

A food combining Christmas can enhance your enjoyment and free you from some of the indigestion and other problems of over-indulgence. See the Christmas menu on page 253.

❦ CHAPTER 6 ❦
Diets for Life Stages

• Pregnancy •

The food combining diet is ideal for pregnancy because it returns control of diet to the appetite mechanism and allows the natural development of pregnancy, with its hormonal and physical changes.

Resist all cravings that take you outside the food combining diet, but ensure that your diet is as broad as possible. Eat one protein meal every day, and fill up at starch and vegetable meals if you are still hungry.

You are unlikely to put on excess weight while following the food combining diet and maintaining your regular exercise programme.

You should maintain a higher intake of fat, particularly from oily fish, and of dairy fat – cream and butter in moderation. It may be wise to avoid processed fat such as margarines and low-fat spreads, until the health effects of these are clearer.

Pregnant women should not eat liver, because the high vitamin A levels can be toxic.

• Feeding Baby: Breast or Bottle •

Human mothers' milk is ideal for babies. Nutrients are produced in the right quantities and in the right form for the human baby to absorb. Mother's milk also provides antibodies which help protect against infection, it is at the right temperature and at the right concentration. There is not the same risk of infection from equipment or contaminated water supplies. Ideally a mother should breast-feed for at least six months.

In a very few cases proteins from food are transported intact into the mother's milk and can cause a reaction in the baby. A baby with the coeliac condition (see page 59) may react to gluten from wheat in the mother's diet. Others may react to protein from cow's milk, and, very rarely, to protein from nuts.

A breast-feeding mother should ensure that she has a diet rich in magnesium. Good sources are nuts, raisins and sultanas, bananas and soya products. If she eats two meals based on starch and fruit or vegetables, and one protein meal each day, she should not lack any nutrients.

Formula milks based on modified cow's milk must be made up to the exact concentration. A baby's kidneys can be immature and unable to excrete the waste products if there is insufficient liquid in the diet. Unmodified cow's milk contains too much phosphorus (as phosphates) for human infants and the calcium may be bonded to the fat and not properly absorbed. This can result in low blood calcium levels and a risk of muscular spasms. Cow's milk is also particularly low in copper and iron.

Solid foods should not be introduced before four months old and wheat should be avoided until the infant is nine months to a year old.

Start by introducing a purée of fruit or vegetables, served cold or just warm, after the milk feed. This can be mashed ripe banana, apple, pear, or a purée of carrots, potatoes, leeks, cauliflower, parsnips or brown rice. The vegetables should be steamed until cooked with the minimum of water, and should be freshly prepared for each meal. Keep the meals simple, do not mix all the flavours together, and allow the young child time to taste and play with the new sensation of food.

Avoid giving the young child any highly flavoured or spiced food, and do not add salt or sugar when cooking or making the purée. Salt should not be added to infant diets as they cannot excrete the excess. Avoid also manufactured sauces and spreads, such as tomato sauce which have a very high salt and sugar content.

When the young child starts to make chewing movements, small soft lumps of food can be included, but not hard foods like peanuts, on which the child may choke. A stick of carrot or apple should be given to the child to chew on, rather than a rusk.

Young children between the ages of nine months and three and a half years often absorb iron poorly from their food. Separating starch meals from protein meals should greatly improve their iron uptake.

Protein meals for the infant can include cooked egg yolk and very finely minced or shredded meat. A small amount of easily digested pulses, such as lentils, can be included, but avoid the hard-to-digest kidney and soya beans.

• Toddlers to School Age •

Young children need concentrated sources of energy in their food. Whole milk rather than reduced-fat milk should be given to children aged one to two years, and those under five years should *not* be given skimmed milk.

From the age of one year most children can eat a very similar diet to that of adults, but you should still not add salt or extra sugar to their food.

Try to base their meals on a breakfast of starch and fruit, a lunch of starch and vegetables and an evening meal of protein and vegetables. Do not feed them added fibre or high-fibre cereals. The extra fibre will fill them up without nourishing them, and will interfere with the uptake of minerals from their food. Wholegrain rice, wholemeal bread, potatoes in their skins and fresh fruit and vegetables will provide plenty of fibre.

Food should not be smothered in extra fat, but neither should it be removed from their diet. It is still an important source of energy and fat-soluble vitamins.

• School Children •

Children who are active and growing rapidly need more nutrients in proportion to their body size than most adults. They have large appetites because they need the extra food. Resist the temptation to let them fill up on biscuits, sweets, crisps, pastry, chips and soft drinks, but encourage them to eat a broad range of fresh fruit and vegetables. The advice about not adding extra fibre still applies. A good diet will provide more than enough fibre. Try and follow the same pattern of meals as for younger children, with starch and fruit for breakfast, starch and vegetables for lunch and protein, vegetables and fruit for the evening meal

Packed lunches can easily be based on bread and butter, starch spreads and fresh fruit. Children should always be encouraged to select what they want from a small range of choices, and prepare their own packed meal.

As the school child becomes an adolescent it is still important to encourage good, well-balanced eating habits and healthy exercise. There is increasing evidence that adolescents require such exercise in order to lay down the muscle and bone structure that will carry them through their adult lives.

A girl who becomes pregnant before reaching full maturity runs a particularly high risk of suffering from nutritional deficiencies, as her own body's resources are robbed to provide the nutrients for the baby.

• Healthy Adult Diets •

The average diet is too high in protein, fats and sugar, too highly processed and refined, and too salty! It totally disrupts the natural mechanisms that tell us when we have eaten enough.

A healthy adult diet derives most of its energy from starchy foods, fruit and vegetables, with sufficient protein to provide for growth and repair of tissue.

The appetite mechanisms work on starch meals and on protein meals to ensure the delicate balance between the food we need and the food we eat. Unfortunately for eaters of the average diet, the appetite mechanisms do not work on the fat content of refined and processed foods. Even a small imbalance can result in a steady increase in weight and the laying down of body fat. It can also result in the eating disorders of anorexia and bulimia.

If you follow the food combining rules of separating starch and protein meals, and not adding extra fats and sugar to the diet, the natural appetite mechanisms can return to control how much we eat, without the need for us to make a deliberate effort to control body weight.

Some energy is needed just to stay alive. A sleeping man requires 0.3 MJ (megajoules)/hour just to maintain the life processes, and any waking activity that allows the body to rest completely uses slightly more energy. Sitting up at a desk to work will use 0.42 MJ/hour. Light domestic work, washing and dressing, about 0.75 MJ/hour. Active physical work, carrying loads and using shovels or other manual labour, can use 1MJ/hour. Similar energy levels are required for sports activities, but the particularly high-energy requirements of games such as squash – at 2MJ/hour – can be sustained for only a short time.

A lighter and fitter person will require slightly less energy for the same amount of exercise and, on average, a woman requires slightly less energy than a man for the same work.

• High-Energy/Sports Diets •

The most efficient strategy to adopt for any exercise programme is a gradual build-up over several weeks. All the body systems, not just the muscles, need to be brought gradually to a state of fitness. There is no need to increase protein intake to build muscle, as most of the protein that you eat will simply be destroyed, putting an extra load on the kidneys.

Keep to a breakfast of starch and fruit (without added sugar) and a lunch of starch and vegetables (without too much added fat) and a single protein meal each day.

If you find your appetite increasing with the extra exercise, add to the starch in your meals, not the protein and not extra fat. If you are to engage in prolonged heavy exercise, such as hard manual labour, for more than eight hours each day, you may even require three starch-based meals a day, plus the one protein meal. But do resist the temptation to cover the starch with fat or sugar.

For intensive occasional exercise the body is dependent on mobilizing reserves already in place, rather than deriving them from food immediately before or during the exercise. Training over several weeks ensures that this mobilization of reserves takes place efficiently and is less likely to cause the highs and low of blood sugar that result from high sugar and fat diets. Any food remaining in the stomach will reduce the body's capacity to participate in intensive exercise. Do not eat a fatty meal any closer than four hours before vigorous exercise. A protein meal requires at least two hours for digestion before starting vigorous exercise and a starch meal one hour.

The food combining diet, together with proper training, results in a person who is much fitter and able to enjoy all sporting activities.

• Medium-Energy Diets •

There is a simple balance for each person between the food they eat, the exercise they take and whether they gain or lose weight. It is important to remember that this differs widely from person to person. Do not eat spoon-for-spoon with someone else in your family, or circle of friends, just because they can eat large meals and not put on weight.

If your weight is increasing:

a) you need to take more exercise
b) you need to eat less
c) you may be pregnant (if female).

Adjusting your food combining diet to match your energy needs is straightforward. If your weight continues to show a steady rise, but you are getting sufficient exercise, check first of all that you are not still eating biscuits, crisps and cakes. These are the biggest source of hidden fat and sugar in our diet.

Check that you are not adding too much fat in butter, margarine, oils or spreads and dressings to your meals. Remember that a spoonful of fat contains twice as much energy as a spoonful of starch. Are you eating too much fat with your protein meal? Stick to lean cuts of meat, like chicken.

If you have checked all these items and your weight still increases, then slowly reduce the starch content of one of your meals – you can add extra salad or green vegetables to compensate, but don't be tempted to add extra dressings as well!

The lowest energy requirements can be satisfied by one meal of fresh fruit, one meal of starch and vegetables and one meal of protein and vegetables.

Provided you don't eat snacks between meals, you will soon find that your natural appetite mechanisms re-establish themselves on this diet and you won't need to calculate your energy requirements. You will find yourself eating what you need.

• Dieting for Weight Loss •

Do not try to lose weight rapidly except under medical supervision. Rapid weight loss can result in an even greater imbalance of the body's metabolism and can have some nasty side-effects.

Aim to lose weight gently. Set a target of months, rather than weeks or days, and adopt a regime that you know you can keep to. A weight loss of 1 lb/450 g a week is probably better than 2 1b/1 kg a week, and don't try to lose more.

Food combining produces ideal weight-loss diets because it is based on normal, healthy and tasty foods.

Let us assume you are obtaining sufficient exercise (because weight loss without exercise results in loss of protein from muscle – your body will keep the fat!). Aim to build up from a minimum of three twenty-minute periods of exercise each week to at least three thirty-minute periods a week, and if possible a thirty-minute exercise period every day.

Let us also assume that you have removed cakes, biscuits, crisps, fried food and fatty meat from your diet. If you haven't done so yet, don't cut out all your favourite unhealthy foods at one go, but reduce them slowly so that you can adjust to the change more easily. And don't cut out fat altogether. At least 20 per cent of your energy should come from fat such as olive oil and oily fish. You should also be allowing yourself only one measure of wine per day (maximum), with your protein meal. Cut all fat and sugar spreads to the absolute minimum, with a small amount of butter *or* jam on your bread.

For breakfast eat fresh, non-starchy fruit, such as apples, pears and oranges, rather than fruit juice. Let your own appetite govern how much to eat, but don't go on eating them for the rest of the morning. Drink water whenever you are thirsty, or weak tea. Don't be tempted to snack mid-morning but wait till lunch time for a starchy meal. Baked potato (eat the skins!) and salad with a thin dressing of olive oil is ideal – but don't soak the potato in butter or other spreads or oils. Brown rice with a mushroom sauce is another tasty alternative. Wholemeal bread is excellent, if you can resist the temptation to cover it with butter or other spreads. Why not try it with a green salad and a thin dressing of olive oil again? But do select a wide variety of meals. A narrow range of ingredients cannot provide a healthy diet.

For your evening meal select a low-fat meat or fish – an oily fish such as herring won't do you any harm – and eat it with plenty of green vegetables. If you are still hungry, fill up with those green vegetables.

Every day that you can follow this diet will help. Don't give up just because you don't manage the food combining diet every day or at every meal. Nobody is that perfect!

Remember that when your weight is approaching your new desirable weight, food combining is the way to keep it there.

It's a diet you can stick with because it's easy to follow and uses healthy ingredients.

• Menopause •

The menopause brings many changes to a woman's body, but the hormonal changes, with their accompanying mood swings, often appear before other signs. As well as the obvious changes brought about by differing levels of the reproductive hormones, serotonin levels in the brain can also change, causing disruption of sleeping patterns and depression, and inducing a lack of self-confidence. These unexpected and unexplained changes are responsible for the disruption of many lives, including broken marriages.

Now some medical studies are showing that the high-starch food combining diet is able to counteract some of these hormonal changes, including boosting serotonin levels and so avoiding the mood swings that accompany them.

The natural fibre associated with the high natural starch levels of wholegrain rice, wholemeal bread and fresh fruit and vegetables seems to play the most important role in safeguarding both the male and female metabolism from unwanted changes. Refined starches with added fibre do not demonstrate any of these desirable properties.

• 60-Plus •

As people age there is a tendency for them to take less exercise and for their body weight to decrease. This starts a vicious circle of loss of appetite and tiredness, followed by less exercise and loss of muscle and bone tissue, leading to the inability to take more exercise.

This must be counteracted by a programme of exercise. There have now been many medical studies, including information from astronauts spending long periods in space, which show that only exercise that puts sufficient stress on the bones will maintain bone weight and muscle strength. If you don't use it, you'll lose it!

The second priority for older people is to ensure that their digestive systems are functioning efficiently and are not put under undue stress. The nutritional requirements of an older person are still similar to those of the younger adult, and the food combining lifestyle will ensure a stress-free digestive system. An active man or very active woman will still require two starch-based meals a day and one protein meal, but fresh fruit and vegetables are just as important for their vitamin and fibre content as for younger people. The aim should be to increase exercise where possible to match these meals, rather than reducing meals to match a low rate of exercise. The 1992 Committee on Medical Aspects of Food Policy recommended that older people should aim to eat meals based on starchy foods. They also particularly recommended oily fish for a protein meal as a source of vitamin D, and because the fish oils reduce the risk of thrombosis.

Regular exercise and the food combining diet should ensure that illness is not so severe, and that recovery from illness or injury is more rapid.

The food combining diet should also minimize the risk of developing diabetes and other age-related digestive disorders. It also helps to maintain the natural hormone levels in the body.

❦ CHAPTER 7 ❦
Special Diets

● Keeping Sugar Levels Low ●

Many populations of people worldwide have shown an explosion of diabetes and other diet-related disorders when they change from their traditional diets to a Western-style diet of refined foods, fat and sugar mixtures, and starch and protein mixtures.

Their traditional diets were often very close to the food combining ideal. Most meals in the week comprised unrefined starchy vegetables, green vegetables and fruit in season. Protein meals were a rarity for most of these populations, as they were able to afford or catch only one or two protein sources per week, and the protein meal would be eaten as a special meal on its own. Such populations often kept their teeth undamaged into old age.

Meals based on unrefined starchy vegetables, green vegetables and fruit are digested sufficiently slowly for there to be no damaging surge of sugars entering the bloodstream. Under these conditions diabetes rarely develops.

The first priority for an individual who may be at risk of developing diabetes is to follow the food combining diet to minimize the possibility of this condition developing and to ensure that they are not overweight, which causes problems in sugar metabolism.

If the condition has already started, the food combining diet offers a strong possibility of preventing it from worsening, or of controlling it by diet alone. Many Asian diabetics keep their blood-sugar levels under control simply because 60 per cent of their diet comprises unrefined rice and pea starch. In severe cases of diabetes, four or five small starch-based meals spread evenly throughout the day may be advised by your doctor.

If you think you are at risk from diabetes, or have already developed the condition, you should follow this diet under the guidance of your doctor or nutritionist. This book is not a substitute for up-to-date medical advice.

• Keeping Fat and Cholesterol Levels Low •

Low-fat diets are often needed to counteract the effects of damage done by highly refined, high-fat, Western diets. Prevention is always better than having to live for the rest of your life with the problems of a damaged digestive system.

The food combining diet, by avoiding much of the fats in the Western diet and the unhealthy sugar/fat mixtures, greatly reduces the chances of damage to the digestive system. The food combining diet is also a naturally low-fat diet. If you are following a low-fat diet for medical reasons, you should discuss your diet with your doctor or nutritionist. If you cut out all the sources of fat in your diet you may end up with a diet that is *too low* in fat.

The main sources of dietary fat are cakes, biscuits and spreads like butter or margarine added to bread. Chocolate, most nuts and nut butters are high in fats, as are all oils, vegetable or otherwise. Remove obvious fat from meat and use chicken or turkey meat without the skin. Don't use full milk, butter or cheese. Use skimmed milk and low-fat yogurt. Avocado is one of the few fruits to be high in fat. Fish like herring and mackerel contain oil, as do trout and salmon, particularly when farmed.

Always cook using moist methods, without adding extra fat, and droplets of fat can be skimmed from the top of cooking liquid before making sauces.

If blood-cholesterol levels are too high, it is more important to cut out the excess fat from your diet than to remove all foods containing cholesterol. Most cholesterol in the blood is manufactured by the liver from surplus fat. Cholesterol from food such as eggs or oily fish has little effect on blood-cholesterol levels. Eggs and oily fish are both valuable additions to the diet.

• Food Allergy and Intolerance •

Wheat and its relatives are the commonest causes of food-induced illness. Lactose, the sugar in milk, is the second biggest cause of problems. As many people leave childhood, the quantity of lactose they can digest is reduced. Any extra is utilized by bacteria in the digestive tract and produces considerable discomfort. Many people suffer from intolerance to other foodstuffs.

A processed diet often makes these problems far worse. The food combining diet helps prevent food allergy and intolerance from developing, by ensuring a diet based on a broad range of foods, and a healthy digestive system; but where problems have arisen, the food combining diet makes it easier to identify and avoid problem foods, because they are not hidden in refined mixtures.

Sending off hair samples for analysis and similar testing methods have no scientific basis. Self-diagnosis of food allergy can also be dangerous. If you exclude a food that causes an allergy, your sensitivity to the food can dramatically increase. If you then reintroduce the food, it can cause a dangerous shock reaction. For this reason, allergy testing should only be done under properly qualified medical supervision.

• Wheat-Free, Gluten-Free Diet •

Many people are unable to tolerate the protein called gluten in wheat, oats, barley or rye. These grains, and any flour or food containing them, should therefore be totally excluded from their diet. Gluten can cause severe indigestion and result in destruction of the villi that absorb food from the small intestine. Other symptoms can range from skin-rash to headaches and general malaise. You should consult a doctor for medical advice if you think you suffer from this, which is known as the coeliac condition.

The wheat-free and gluten-free diet is a diet for life – it cannot be forgotten about. Even a few crumbs of bread in a dip, traces of bread or batter in deep frying oil, or a spoonful of flour to thicken gravy are enough to make life miserable for the coeliac.

The digestive system of the coeliac is often damaged before the condition is brought to the attention of the doctor and diagnosis can take place. The food combining diet, with its sensible balance of unrefined starches, fruit and vegetables, provides the optimal diet for recovery of the digestive system, and for maintaining health in the future.

The easiest way to avoid hidden wheat flour (which gets into almost everything, from mustard powder, baking powder and gravy mixes to ice cream) is to use only pure natural fruit and vegetables, and unprepared cuts of meat. The author speaks from personal experience!

Wheat fibre is also highly abrasive and should not be added to food. Arthritis is also sometimes linked to wheat or other food intolerances.

Most wheat-free and gluten-free ingredients can be obtained from your local supermarket or health food shop. The main importer and miller of these ingredients is Virani Foods, 10–14 Stewarts Road, Finedon Road Industrial Estate, Wellingborough, Northants NN8 4RJ.

• Salt-Free Diet •

There are so many hidden sources of salt in manufactured foods, including breakfast cereals, that salt-free or low-salt diets should be produced from pure natural ingredients. Any menu or recipe based on these ingredients can be used.

Salt should not be added in cooking or baking.

Raising agents should not be used – the problem concerns the sodium ions from both the salt and sodium bicarbonate.

● Sugar-Free Diet ●

Sugar is added to most manufactured foods to improve their attractiveness to children and adults. It can be added to meat products as well as fruit and vegetables. The sugar levels are often disguised by displaying only part as sugar, and quoting levels for dextrose, glucose, glucose syrup, milk sugar and fruit juice – all of which are sugar – as separate items.

Sugar-free diets should be based on fresh meat, fish, wholegrain cereals and green vegetables. Most fruit and root vegetables, including carrots, beetroot and swedes, are relatively high in sugar, but as the sugar is enclosed within the plant cell walls it is released only slowly on digestion.

● Dairy-Free Diet ●

Milk-derived protein, casein, milk sugars, milk fat and other components of milk can be added to a wide range of manufactured foods. There need not be any reference to milk or dairy products on the label.

A dairy-free diet should be based on fresh meat, fish, wholegrain cereals, fruit and fresh vegetables.

● Yeast-Free Diet ●

Yeast-free diets need to avoid natural sources of yeast as well as those added to food. A low-sugar diet is also sensible to prevent natural growth of yeast cells within the digestive system.

Avoid all breads, doughs and cakes that may use yeast as a raising agent, as well as the skins of fresh fruit. Avoid also sugar spreads and jams, which often contain yeasts.

❦ CHAPTER 8 ❦
Food Lists and Ingredients

All too often, the Western diet is based on wheat, or wheat/rice/maize. As the following list shows, a wide variety of starchy foods are available in the supermarkets. A healthy diet should be based on a broad range of these starchy foods. These lists also show the wide range of protein foods now available. A broad range of foods in the diet should always be the aim of the menu planner.

* indicates foods which are high in calcium and potassium salts (the alkaline earth elements)

• Starch Food List •

Amaranth
Arrow root
Artichoke – Jerusalem
Breadfruit
Buckwheat, Kasha
Carob flour
Cassava
Cornmeal
Cornflour – avoid refined
Maize
* Millet flake and flour
Pasta
Potato
Quinnoa

Rice and rice flour
Sago – avoid refined
Sorghum and sorghum flour
Spaghetti
* Sweet chestnut flour
Sweet potato
Tapioca, cassava, manioc
* Teff
Wheat
Wild rice
Yam

The following sweeteners can be used in moderation with starch meals:
* Black treacle
Honey
Maple syrup
* Molasses

• Protein Food List •

* Eggs
Meat
Beef, mutton, lamb, pork
Chicken, goose, duck
Kidney
Liver
Rabbit, hare, turkey, venison
Veal
* Cheese
* Fromage frais
* Yogurt
Fish and other sea food
* Herring, mackerel, sardine
Salmon and trout
Brill, halibut, turbot
Cod, coley, haddock, hake, pollack, whiting

Sole, plaice, dab and flounder
Tuna, swordfish
Cartilaginous fish
Dogfish
Ray and skate
Shark
Molluscs
Bivalve molluscs, oysters
Mussels
Crustaceans
Lobster, crab
Prawns and shrimps
* Soya
* Tofu – soya curd

● Fruit to Eat on Its Own or with a Protein Meal ●

Apple
Apricot
Avocado
Bilberry
* Blackcurrant and redcurrant
Bramble, blackberry
Carambola, star fruit
Cherry – morello
Cherry – sweet
* Citrus fruit: orange, lemon, tangerine, grapefruit and lime
Cranberry – not liked by Dr Hay
Gooseberry
Grape
Guava
Kiwi fruit
Lime
Loquat
Lychee
Mango
Melon – on its own – Dr Hay

Passion fruit
Pawpaw, papaya – only with meal
Peach
Persimmon, date plum
Pineapple – fresh only with meal
Plum – not liked by Dr Hay
Prune
Raspberry
Rhubarb – only to the end of May
* Strawberry
* Tomato

● Fruit to Eat on Its Own or with a Starch Meal ●

Banana
Custard apple
* Date
* Fig, fresh or dried
Grape
Pear
* Raisin
* Sultana

● Vegetables that Go with Any Meal ●

Alfalfa
Artichoke – globe
Asparagus
Aubergine
Beetroot
* Brassicas: cabbage, sprouts, cauliflower, kohlrabi, pak choi, pe-tsai
Broad bean
Carrot
Cayenne pepper and chilli
Celeriac

* Celery
Cucumber
Endive
Fennel
Garlic
Horseradish
Leek
Lentil
Lettuce
Marrow, Squash
Nasturtium
Onion
Parsley
* Parsnip
Peas – fresh
Pumpkin
Runner bean – scarlet
* Spinach
Sweet corn
Turnip and swede

● Herbs and Spices that Go with Any Meal ●

A sprinkling of herbs and spices adds flavour and variety to meals as well as providing some extra trace elements, minerals and vitamins.

Don't overdo it, though. Some herbs are harmful in larger amounts.

Allspice should be ground, as and when required, from the whole sun-dried berries. Use it in marinades, pickles, mulled wine, chocolate drinks and to flavour both sweet and savoury dishes.

Anise, star is used ground into a spice to flavour savoury dishes.

Aniseed is grey-green when fresh, going grey when stale. Grind immediately before use, to flavour bread and cakes.

Basil is an excellent herb for salads and savoury dishes.

Bay leaves can be used whole to flavour stews, soups and casseroles for both fish and meat dishes.

Borage flowers and leaves are another useful addition to salads.

Capers are small, pickled flower buds that can be used in cold sauces or with pizza.

Caraway seed can be added to bread, cakes, fruit, salads and vegetable dishes.

Cardamom pods are best used whole to flavour rice and pulse dishes, or the seed can be freshly ground to flavour cakes and bread.

Chervil leaves can be added to soups, salads and omelettes.

Cinnamon bark is difficult to grind and is best purchased as a powder. It can be used to flavour bread, cakes, fruit, rice and curries.

Cloves have a strong flavour. The dried whole bud can be crumbled to flavour cakes or fruit. They can also be used in marinades, casseroles, gravies and mulled wine.

Coriander leaves can be added to salad, and the seeds should be lightly roasted before adding to stews, casseroles and curries or vegetable dishes.

Cumin seed should also be roasted before use in curry.

Dill leaves can be eaten in salads and the seed in bread and cakes.

Fennel can be cooked as a vegetable and the aniseed flavour goes well with fish.

Fenugreek leaves are used to flavour curry and dhal, and the seeds can be roasted before grinding as an addition to curry powder.

Ginger is easiest to use fresh. The dried root has to be crushed with a mallet before use. It can be added to bread and cakes as well as savoury dishes and curries.

Lovage leaves can be used to flavour soups and salads.

Mace should be purchased in small amounts as it does not keep well. Use it to flavour sweet and savoury dishes that include milk.

Nutmeg seeds should be grated as required. Only a pinch should be used, as it is poisonous in quantity. It is used to flavour cakes, custards and fruit.

Paprika varies from a mild sweetness to a hot and fiery ingredient of curries. Purchase in small amounts and use with care to flavour savoury dishes.

Pepper should be freshly ground for the best flavour, and added to savoury dishes towards the end of the cooking period.

Peppermint leaves can be added to fruit salads.

Poppy seeds should be roasted, before crushing and adding to bread, cakes, vegetables or sauces.

Sage leaves can be added to stuffings, soups and stews.

Savory, the leaves of both summer and winter varieties, can be used to flavour stews and savoury dishes.

Tarragon leaves can be used in salads and savoury dishes.

Thyme leaves can also be used in salads and savoury dishes.

Vanilla pods can be used several times by steeping the pod in the liquid of the dish for an hour, and then removing the pod and drying for reuse.

• Dried Beans and Peas •

Most peas and beans can be sprouted and used as a vitamin-rich vegetable with any meal.

Dried peas and beans are indigestible and need careful cooking, although they are an important source of protein for vegans. Use only in small amounts with protein meals (less than 1 oz/25 g per person).

* high in calcium and potassium salts
  * Azuki or aduki bean
  * Blackeye bean, cow pea, kafir-bean, yard bean
  * Butter bean or lima bean
  * Chick pea, bengal gram, besan flour, garbanzo
  * French, kidney or haricot bean
  * Gram flour
  * Mung bean
  * Pigeon pea, red gram
  * Peanut

• Nuts and Seeds that Go with a Protein Meal •

* high in calcium and potassium salts
    * Almond
    * Brazil nut
    * Cashew
    Coconut
    * Hazelnut
    * Pecan
    * Pine nut
    * Pistachio
    * Pumpkin seed
    * Sesame
    * Sunflower
    * Walnut
    Water chestnut

• Nuts and Seeds that Go with a Starch Meal •

* high in calcium and potassium salts
    Coconut
    * Hazelnut
    * Pecan
    Sweet chestnut
    * Walnut

• Oils and Fats that Go with Any Meal •

in moderation only
* high in calcium and potassium salts
    Butter
    * Cream
    * Milk
    Olives
    Olive oil

Rapeseed oil
Safflower oil
All unrefined nut and seed oils (groundnut oil and peanut oil
are two names for the same oil).

• Sugars •

With the exception of honey, molasses or maple syrup in small
amounts, no refined sugars add any useful nutrients to the diet.
The energy provided by sugar is far better coming from
unrefined starch. Fruit juices can also provide unnaturally
high levels of sugar. It makes much more nutritional sense
to eat the fruit, not the processed juice. Artificial sweeteners are
also best avoided.

• Chocolate •

Chocolate is a mixture of fat and sugar and you should restrict
as far as possible. Use only for special occasions, for example.

	protein	starch	sugar	fat	water or non-starch fibre	calcium/100g
Chocolate	8.4%	2.9%	56.5%	30.3%	1.9%	220mg

• Oils and Fats: Butter, Olives, Olive Oil •

Oils and fats are the most concentrated energy food in our diet.
   The 1994 review of nutritional aspects of heart disease
suggest a *maximum* proportion of energy from fat of 35 per
cent of the dietary energy intake, and a maximum of 10 per cent
from saturated fat. The optimum level is much lower than this,
but a very low-fat diet is equally unhealthy.

Butter is made by separating the milk fat from the liquid. It is 80 per cent fat and contains no protein. It should not be excluded from the diet, as it is an excellent natural source of vitamin E.

	protein	starch	sugar	fat	calcium/100g
Butter	0.5%			81.7%	15mg
Olive oil				91.4%	
Sunflower oil				99.9%	
Nut butter	22.6%	6.4%	6.7%	53.7%	37mg
Margarine	0.2%		1%	81.6%	4mg

• Coffee, Tea •

Both can be drunk in moderation. Coffee is a powerful stimulant, but it is also an irritant to the digestive system. The tannins in tea can also interfere with mineral uptake from the food and cause staining of the teeth.

• Other Ingredients •

Sodium bicarbonate adds sodium to the diet, and the quantity used should be kept to the minimum needed as a raising agent.

Salt (sodium chloride) is easy to add in excess to your diet. Don't add salt to cooking water, as it reduces the quality of the nutrients available in vegetables. Add only the minimum quantity needed to your plate.

Salt should not be added to the food of young children, and they should not be given salted chips or other foods high in salt, as their kidneys are unable to excrete the excess.

PART 2
Recipes

❦ CHAPTER 9 ❦
Starch Recipes

• The Main Starch Grains: Wheat, Oats, Barley, Rye, Maize •

Wheat is known to have been used in ancient Egypt, Greece and Rome, but white wheat flour remained a luxury food item for the rich until 1800. The wheat grain has a store of starch, the endosperm; the embryo, which is also known as the wheat germ; and the bran, testa and aleurone layers, which surround the whole grain.

To make white wheat flour, the wheat germ and the bran, testa and aleurone layers are removed, taking with them 98 per cent of the available thiamine and 90 per cent of the available niacin, pyridoxine and pantothenic acids. Flour is white because of the addition of bleaching agents and chemicals, which age the flour. The food combining diet suggests that unbleached and much more nutritious wholemeal flours should be used instead. Wholemeal bread is an excellent staple food.

Pasta is made from durum wheat, ground into semolina and then made into a paste with water. The dough is made into a variety of shapes and then dried. The dry pasta will keep for up to a year. Some pasta dough is made from wholemeal flour and some includes egg.

Oats contain a much softer fibre than wheat and the grain is more easily digested, making it a very nutritious cereal. Oats make an excellent breakfast cereal and can be added to many other starchy dishes. They can help to reduce high cholesterol levels.

Barley is hardier than wheat and has been used in the cooler regions of Europe and Asia since Neolithic times. Barley cakes can be made in a similar way to oat cakes.

Rye will grow in much colder climates than the other grains but is prone to fungal infection. It makes a dark and heavy bread.

Maize was originally cultivated in the American continent and has the poorest nutritional balance of these cereals. This can be improved by boiling the grain in a 5 per cent lime solution before grinding it to a flour – a process used in the making of tortillas. Polenta is a partly cooked maize meal. Cornflour is almost pure corn starch and has little other nutritional value, except for a wheat-free diet.

Bread purchased in a shop will contain added calcium and will have many of the vitamins returned to it. It may also contain preservatives to extend its shelf life. Fresh bread does not need a fat spread over it, so keep any layer of butter as thin as possible.

Breakfast cereals do not always make a healthy start to the day. Many brands have too much salt and sugar, and the dry-heat method of processing can make some of the starch indigestible. A few brands also have a high fat content. Cornflakes often have nutrients added in the manufacturing process. Home-made mueslis based on oatflakes can, however, provide a healthy mix of ingredients at an attractive price.

	protein	starch	sugar	fat	calcium/100g
Wheat, whole	12.7%	75.6%	2.1%	1.3%	41mg
Oats	11.2%	64.9%	1.1%	9.2%	52mg
Barley	8.2%	78.8%		1%	
Rye	12.1%	73.4%		1.7%	38mg
Maize	7.8%	76.8%		2.6%	20mg

• The Main Starch Grains: Rice, Millet and Sorghum •

Wholegrain brown rice is much more nutritious than white rice, as many of rice's nutrients are found in the brown layer immediately below the skin of the grain. Rice is best cooked by boiling, but as some of the nutrients are water-soluble, this water should not be discarded but used to make a sauce or kept for a starchy soup. Brown rice is also an excellent source of fibre. Short-grain types of rice cook to a soft texture, and although commonly reserved for puddings, are equally useful for savoury dishes. The long-grain rices are drier and firmer when cooked. Basmati rice is slightly chewier to the bite.

Rice can be purchased parboiled and then dried again. This has a slightly higher nutritional value than white rice, but it is as easy to cook. Wholegrain brown rice can also be purchased parboiled which considerably reduces the cooking time.

Millet is a group of highly nutritious, small-seeded tropical grains. It has the highest protein level of any cereal and is also excellent for providing potassium and magnesium. The better-quality grains are larger and greener than the round-seeded yellow grains. Millet can be cooked in the same way as rice, but it tends to need longer to cook and will absorb more water. The small grains can also be ground to make a millet porridge. Millet flakes are a useful and healthy addition to muesli.

Sorghum is a larger grain than millet and is a staple of the hot, dry regions of Africa and Asia. It is another highly nutritious and easily digested cereal, which is often used to make baby foods. It can be used for baking, mixed with wheat flour.

	protein	starch	sugar	fat	calcium/100g
Rice, brown	7.5%	77%	0.5%	1.9%	4mg
Millet	12%	69%			+++
Sorghum	11%	73%		3.3%	+++

+++ a good source, but accurate figures not available.

• Other Starchy Grains and Flours: Amaranth, Buckwheat, Quinnoa, Teff, Wild Rice •

Amaranth was an important food crop of the Aztec civilization and is now cultivated in small quantities worldwide. It is easily digested and contains a good balance of nutrients.

Buckwheat was first cultivated in the cooler regions of China. The hard husks are removed from the grain before sale. It is known in Russia as *kasha* and used to make strong-flavoured porridge and pancakes, or it can be cooked in the same way as rice.

Quinnoa is a native of Peru. The small seed is highly nutritious, but contains bitter saponins. The grain should be washed in boiling water before use. It can be cooked as rice (although it cooks much more quickly) or ground into flour to make bread.

Teff is another highly nutritious small grain, a staple crop of Ethiopia. It is used to make porridge or pancakes.

Wild rice is a wetland plant of North America, but it is difficult to harvest, and its price is high. It can be cooked in the same way as rice, often being used to decorate a rice dish.

	protein	starch+sugar	fat	calcium/100g
Amaranth	15%	63%	7%	490mg
Buckwheat	8–10%	62%		114mg

• Starchy Roots and Tubers: Potato, Sweet Potato, Jerusalem Artichoke, Yam •

The **potato** is a valuable source of easily digested starch, but the main other nutrients are found in the outer layer, immediately below the skin. Peeling a potato therefore destroys its nutritional value, as does baking a potato, if the skin is then burnt or discarded. Potatoes should be scrubbed clean and then boiled until just soft, or baked, without burning the skin. The skin should be eaten as well as the starchy middle. The green skin and flesh that develops when a potato is exposed to the light should be discarded, as it is poisonous.

Sweet potatoes include more sugar and twice as much Vitamin C as ordinary potatoes but do not keep well. They are usually cooked by boiling and mashing, but are also excellent when baked.

Jerusalem artichokes taste sweet because of a sugar called insulin. They can be cooked in the same way as a potato.

Yams are the tubers of tropical climbing plants, an important source of starch in parts of Africa, but they contribute little more to the diet.

	protein	starch	sugar	fat	calcium/100g
Potato	3.9%	30.5%	1.2%	0.2%	11mg
Sweet potato	1.1%	8.9%	11.6%	0.3%	23mg
Yam	1.7%	32.3%	0.7%	0.3%	12mg

● Starchy Fruit: Breadfruit, Banana Plantain, Water Chestnut, Sweet Chestnut ●

Breadfruit is a large, starchy fruit, used before it is fully ripe. The flesh is served boiled and mashed, or cut into slices and roasted. Never eat it raw. The seeds can also be roasted. The dried flesh can be used as a flour.

Plantains contain more starch than other bananas and can be cooked as a vegetable. Banana flour is sometimes produced from plantains and used in the manufacture of baby foods.

Water chestnuts are starchy nuts that were an important source of food in Europe in Neolithic times. They can be cooked by boiling or made into bread.

Sweet chestnuts are an important crop of southern Europe, and a staple food in some parts of Italy and France. They can be boiled and used as a vegetable, used as a purée or made into a flour for bread or pancakes. They are rich in many nutrients. They have the highest sugar content of any nut.

	protein	starch	sugar	fat	calcium/100g
Plantain	0.8%	23%	5.5%	0.2%	5mg

Starches of little nutritional value

Most refined starches have little to offer the food combining diet. These include cornflour, corn starch, potato starch, as well as sago and tapioca (manioc, cassava).

• Banana, Date, Sultana •

None of these fruits contain any quantity of starch, but they store sugar within the cellulose cell wall, which prevents the surge of sugar that comes from refined sugar in the diet. They form a useful sweetener for starchy meals, but this should not form more than 20 per cent of the ingredients by weight.

They all contain useful amounts of calcium and potassium.

	protein	starch	sugar	fat	calcium/100g
Banana	1.2%	2.3%	20.9%	0.3%	11mg
Date	0.9%		11.5%	0.1%	13mg
Sultana	2.7%		69.4%	0.4%	64mg

Starch Breads

Wholemeal Bread

Makes two 1 lb/450 g loaves
¾ pint/450 ml warm water
1 oz/25 g fresh yeast or ½ oz/15 g dried yeast
1 teaspoon castor sugar
1½ lb/680 g wholemeal flour
2 level teaspoons sea salt

- Pour the water into a bowl and add the yeast and sugar.

- Leave for about 15 minutes until frothy.

- Sift flour and salt into a bowl, make a well in the centre and add the yeast liquid.

- Mix to a soft dough.

- Knead until the dough is smooth and elastic – about 10 minutes by hand or 2 minutes in a food mixer.

- Shape into loaves and brush with salt water, then cover with a damp cloth or oiled polythene bag and leave to rise for 1½ hours. (Some dried yeasts will rise more quickly.)

- Bake at gas mark 8, 450°F, 230°C for 25–35 minutes. Turn out and cool on a wire rack.

Variations

- Sprinkle sesame seeds or poppy seeds over the top before baking.

- Add 1 oz/25 g butter or lard and rub into the flour.

- The best results are obtained with 'strong' flour milled from hard wheats. You may need to use more liquid.

Wheat Soda Bread

Makes one large loaf
8 oz/225 g white flour
8 oz/225 g wholemeal flour
1½ teaspoons bicarbonate of soda
1 tablespoon olive oil
1 teaspoon salt
¾ pint/450 ml warm water

- Mix the flours, bicarbonate of soda, olive oil and salt in a bowl, make a well in the centre and add the water.

- Mix to a soft dough – add more water if required.

- Knead until the dough is smooth and elastic – about 10 minutes by hand or 2 minutes in a food mixer.

- Shape into a round loaf on a floured board and then place on a baking tray.

- Bake at gas mark 6, 400°F, 200°C for 25–35 minutes. Turn out and cool on a wire rack.

Variations

- Sprinkle sesame seeds or poppy seeds over the top before baking.

- Stand a bowl of water in the oven to give the steamy atmosphere needed for a good crust.

- You can use all wholemeal flour, but this will produce a heavier loaf.

Wholemeal Pizza Base

Makes a pizza for 4 people
1 oz/25 g fresh yeast or 1 tablespoon dried yeast +1 teaspoon sugar
¼ pint/150 ml warm milk
½ oz/15 g lard
8 oz/225 g wholemeal flour
salt to taste
non-protein topping of your choice (see below)

- Crumble the fresh yeast into the liquid or mix in the dried yeast and sugar. Keep warm until the yeast is working well.

- Rub the lard into the flour with the salt.

- Slowly mix the flour into the liquid until a uniform dough is formed.

- Knead for 1 minute into a stiff dough.

- Roll the dough out to form a 12 in/30 cm circle and place on a greased baking tray.

- Leave to rise in a warm place for 30 minutes.

- Add the non-protein topping.

- Leave in a warm place for a further 30 minutes.

- Bake in a preheated oven, gas mark 7, 425°F, 220°C for 20–25 minutes.

- Serve hot.

Mixed vegetable topping: onion, mushroom, tomato, courgette, aubergine, all well chopped.

Curried fruit topping: grapes, sultanas, peach slices, onion, tomato, curry sauce to taste. All well chopped.

Mixed Grain Bread

Makes one large loaf
4 oz/100 g white wheat flour
4 oz/100 g wholemeal flour
4 oz/100 g maize flour
4 oz/100 g rice flour
1½ teaspoons bicarbonate of soda
1 tablespoon olive oil
1 teaspoon salt
¾ pint/450 ml warm water

- Mix the flours, bicarbonate of soda, olive oil and salt in a bowl, make a well in the centre and add the water.

- Mix to a soft dough – add more water if required.

- Grease a baking tin. The dough should be almost soft enough to pour into the tin.

- Bake at gas mark 6, 400°F, 200°C for 25–35 minutes. Turn out and cool on a wire rack.

- Check that the loaf is cooked by inserting a skewer through the middle. The loaf is not cooked until the skewer comes out clean.

Variations

- Use millet flour in place of rice flour if you have a grain mill.

- Stand a bowl of water in the oven to give the steamy atmosphere needed for a good crust.

- Experiment by adding a range of herbs to the dough.

Millet and Banana Flat Bread

Staple breads can be made from many other grains, not just wheat. These are traditionally made as flat breads, using millet, sorghum, teff or maize. Before cooking, the mixture is a batter rather than a dough, and the bread is cooked in a flat tray, not a bread tin. The millet and sorghum breads have a much better nutritional balance than wheat breads. The added banana or carrot and egg make a softer, less crumbly bread.

Makes one 1 lb/450 g loaf
1 large banana or 4 oz/100 g grated carrot
½ pint/300 ml water
2 eggs
4 oz/100 g millet or sorghum flour
4 oz/100 g rice flour or ground rice
1 teaspoon bicarbonate of soda
½ teaspoon cream of tartar
¼ teaspoon tartaric acid
1 fl oz/30 ml olive oil
salt to taste

- Beat the banana/carrot to a smooth purée with the water and eggs.

- Mix all the dry ingredients together with the olive oil.

- Fold the flour mixture into the purée.

- Do not overmix. It's easy to knock the gas out of the mixture and produce a heavy bread.

- Line a 10 inch/25 cm square tray with non-stick baking parchment and spread the mixture 1 inch/2.5 cm deep or use greased individual pattie trays.

- Bake in a preheated oven, gas mark 7, 425°F, 220°C for 35–40 minutes.

- Serve hot from the oven.

Oat Bread

Makes two 1 lb/450 g loaves
¼ pint/150 ml warm milk
¼ pint/150 ml warm water
1 oz/25 g fresh yeast or 1 tablespoon dried yeast +1 teaspoon sugar
8 oz/225 g wholemeal flour
8 oz/225 g plain white flour
8 oz/225 g fine oatmeal
4 fl oz/120 ml olive oil
1 oz/25 g molasses
salt to taste

- Mix the milk and water together, crumble the fresh yeast into the liquid or mix in the dried yeast and sugar. Keep warm until the yeast is working well.

- Mix all the dry ingredients together. Then mix in the oil and molasses.

- Slowly mix the flour into the liquid until a uniform dough is formed.

- Knead for 10–15 minutes into a stiff dough.

- Leave in a warm place for 1 hour, when it should double in bulk.

- Knead again for 1 minute and then place in two greased trays.

- Cover the dough with an oiled polythene sheet and keep warm until the dough has risen again.

- Bake in a preheated oven, gas mark 7, 425°F, 220°C for 45 minutes or until done (check with a skewer).

- Turn out of the trays and cool on a wire rack.

Rotla (Millet Flat Bread)

Rotla are the traditional millet flour (*bajri*) breads of the hot, dry regions of the world. They are more nutritious than wheat breads, but are more difficult to make. The millet flour should be fresh. Make only one rotla at a time. Don't try mixing a larger quantity.

Makes 1 rotla
1 fl oz/30 ml freshly boiled water
2 oz/50 g fresh millet flour

- Add the hot water to the flour, a tablespoon at a time, mixing it in well and kneading it heavily as soon as it will stick together.

- Knead the dough until it is smooth – a couple of minutes.

- Press the ball of dough between two sheets of oiled polythene on a board – use a heavy saucepan – until the dough is flattened into a 6 inch/15 cm diameter circle.

- Heat a heavy-based frying pan until it is hot. Do not add oil.

- Cook the rotla for 4 minutes, turning several times. It should become slightly puffy with brown patches.

- Serve hot from the pan.

Variations

- Use barley flour instead of millet flour. This makes the *koda rotla* of the Himalayas.

- Use a mixture of corn meal, rice flour and oatmeal instead of millet flour.

Parathas

Parathas are the staple bread of northern India, quick to make, and best eaten hot from the pan.

Makes enough for 4 people
3 tablespoons olive oil
8 oz/225 g wholemeal flour
¼ pint/150 ml warm water
salt to taste
1 tablespoon melted butter
extra frying oil

- Rub the oil into the flour with the salt.

- Mix in the warm water to form a dough.

- Knead the dough for 5 minutes.

- Divide the dough into 8 portions.

- Roll out each ball on a lightly floured board until 5 inches/12 cm diameter. Brush the top surface with melted butter, fold in half and roll again.

- Fold in half and roll again.

- Heat a heavy-based frying pan until hot. Add a little oil.

- Cook one paratha at a time, for 30 seconds each side. Add a little more frying oil round the edges as you turn the paratha – until they turn brown in places.

Puris (Deep-Fried Puff Bread)

It is important that deep-frying fat is hot, otherwise the dough will absorb too much fat and become soggy. Take care with hot fat. Use a large pan with a small amount of oil and always have a close-fitting lid available for the pan, in case of fire, and never leave hot fat unattended.

Makes 20 puris
2 tablespoons olive oil
8 oz/225 g wholemeal flour
¼ pint/150 ml warm water
deep-frying oil

- Rub the oil into the flour.

- Mix in the warm water to form a dough.

- Knead the dough for 5 minutes.

- Divide the dough into 20 balls.

- Roll out each ball on a lightly floured board until no more than 2 inches/5 cm in diameter.

- Heat the deep-frying oil.

- Cook one puri at a time, for 30 seconds each side – until they puff up and turn golden brown.

Variations

- Flavour the dough with cumin and sesame seeds.

- Stuff the puris with a small quantity of freshly cooked vegetables before frying.

Naan Bread

Naan bread should be eaten fresh and hot. Traditionally it is cooked in a tandoor oven, but a heavy frying pan produces excellent results.

Makes 10–12 naan breads
1 oz/25 g fresh yeast or 1 tablespoon dried yeast +1 teaspoon sugar
½ pint/300 ml warm water
4 fl oz/120 ml olive oil
1 lb/450 g wholemeal flour
salt to taste

- Crumble the fresh yeast into the water or mix in the dried yeast and sugar. Keep warm until the yeast is working well.

- Rub the oil into the flour with the salt.

- Slowly mix the flour into the liquid until a uniform dough is formed.

- Knead for 5 minutes into a stiff dough.

- Leave in a warm place for 1 hour, when it should double in bulk.

- Divide the dough into 12 equal-sized balls.

- Roll out each ball on a lightly floured board until 5 inches/12 cm in diameter. Or slap from hand to hand in the traditional way (not easy!).

- Preheat a heavy-based frying pan. Do not add any oil.

- Cook each naan for 30–40 seconds each side – until brown and puffy in places.

- Serve hot.

Variations

- Mix crushed garlic and chopped fresh coriander into the dough.

- Roll poppy seed or roasted sesame seed into the naan before cooking.

Carrot and Potato Bread

Makes two 1 lb/450 g loaves
½ oz/15 g fresh yeast or ½ tablespoon dried yeast +1 teaspoon sugar
¼ pint/150 ml warm water
12 oz/350 g strong plain white flour
12 oz/350 g wholemeal flour
4 fl oz/120 ml olive oil
salt to taste
4 oz/100 g potato, cooked and mashed
4 oz/100 g carrot, cooked and mashed

- Crumble the fresh yeast into the water or mix in the dried yeast and sugar. Keep warm until the yeast is working well.

- Mix the flours and salt together. Then mix in the oil.

- Mix in the cooked potato and carrot.

- Add the liquid to the flour until a uniform dough is formed.

- Knead for 10–15 minutes into a stiff, smooth dough.

- Cover with an oiled polythene sheet and leave in a warm place for 1–2 hours, when it should double in bulk.

- Knead again for 1 minute and then place in 2 greased tins.

- Cover the dough with an oiled polythene sheet and keep warm until the dough has risen again.

- Bake in a preheated oven, gas mark 5, 375°F, 190°C for 1 hour or until done (check with a skewer – see page 94).

- Turn out of the tins and cool on a wire rack.

- Serve hot.

Variations
- Add a teaspoon of cinnamon or mixed spice to the flour.

Rye Bread

Rye flour, unmixed with wheat flour, makes a very heavy loaf. You can vary the proportions of the two to suit your own tastes, but two-thirds rye flour to one-third wheat flour makes an excellent loaf.

Makes two 1 lb/450 g loaves
¼ pint/150 ml warm milk
¼ pint/150 ml warm water
1 oz/25 g fresh yeast or 1 tablespoon dried yeast +1 teaspoon sugar
1 lb/450 g rye flour
8 oz/225 g strong plain white flour
8 oz/225 g fine oatmeal
salt to taste
4 fl oz/120 ml olive oil or 1 oz/25 g lard
1 oz/25 g molasses

- Mix the milk and water together, crumble the fresh yeast into the liquid or mix in the dried yeast and sugar. Keep warm until the yeast is working well.

- Mix all the dry ingredients together. Then mix in the oil and molasses, or rub in the lard.

- Slowly mix the flour into the liquid until a uniform dough is formed.

- Knead for 10–15 minutes into a stiff dough.

- Cover with an oiled polythene sheet and leave in a warm place for 1 hour, when it should double in bulk.

- Knead again for 1 minute and then place in two greased trays.

- Cover the dough with an oiled polythene sheet and keep warm until the dough has risen again.

- Bake in a preheated oven, gas mark 7, 425°F, 220°C for 45 minutes or until done (check with a skewer – see page 94).

- Turn out of the trays and cool on a wire rack.

Rotli

Makes 8 rotli
2 tablespoons olive oil
8 oz/225 g wholemeal wheat flour
4 fl oz/120 ml warm water

- Rub the oil into the flour in a large bowl.

- Add the water, a little at a time, until a firm dough is produced.

- Knead the dough for 5 minutes.

- Cover with an oiled polythene sheet and leave for 15 minutes.

- Divide the dough into 8 portions.

- Roll out each portion on a floured board until 6 inches/15 cm in diameter.

- Heat a heavy-based frying pan until it is hot. Do not add oil.

- When the pan is hot, cook each rotli for 30–40 seconds each side – until puffy in places and brown spots appear.

- Serve hot with a sauce. (Keep hot in foil lined with kitchen paper.)

Variation

- Add finely sliced onion to each portion of dough as it is rolled out. Fold and then roll out each rotli several times.

Potato Scones

Potato scones are always best served hot from the frying pan with a little butter. A food processor ensures a good mix of potato and flour.

Makes 12 individual scones
1 lb/450 g cooked potato
4 oz/100 g wholemeal flour
salt to taste
1 tablespoon olive oil

- Ensure the potato is well mashed. If you are using a food processor you can include the potato skins.

- Mix the mashed potato, flour, salt and oil together. Work them into a smooth paste.

- Roll the balls of dough out thinly on a lightly floured working surface.

- Heat a lightly oiled heavy frying pan.

- Fry until golden brown each side.

Wholemeal Scones

Scones are always best served hot from the oven with a little butter.

Makes one large scone loaf or 12 individual scones
3 fl oz/85 ml sour milk or cream
½ pint/300 ml warm water
½ oz/15 g fresh yeast or ½ tablespoon dried yeast +1 teaspoon sugar
1 lb/450 g wholemeal flour
1 tablespoon molasses
3 fl oz/85 ml olive oil
salt to taste

- Mix the milk/cream and water together, crumble the fresh yeast into the liquid or mix in the dried yeast and sugar. Keep warm until the yeast is working well.

- Mix the molasses and oil into the flour.

- Slowly mix the flour into the liquid until a uniform dough is formed.

- Knead for 10–15 minutes into a stiff dough.

- Leave in a warm place for 1 hour, when it should double in bulk.

- Form the dough into a ball but don't knead again. Place on a greased tray.

- For individual scones, form the dough into 12 small balls.

- Cover the dough with an oiled polythene sheet and keep warm until the dough has risen again.

- Bake in a preheated oven, gas mark 7, 425°F, 220°C for 45 minutes or until done (check with a skewer – see page 94). Individual scones will not need as long as this – 20–30 minutes should be sufficient.

- Turn out of the trays and cool on a wire rack.

Chestnut Pancakes

Makes 12–16 pancakes
2 eggs
4 oz/100 g sweet-chestnut purée (unsweetened)
8 oz/225 g wholemeal flour
salt to taste
1 teaspoon baking powder
1 tablespoon olive oil
½ pint/300 ml water

- Beat the eggs and the sweet-chestnut purée to a smooth paste – use a food processor.

- Mix the flour, salt, baking powder and olive oil together.

- Mix the egg mixture into the flour mixture and add enough water to form a batter.

- Preheat a heavy-based frying pan.

- Drop the batter into the pan in spoonfuls, and cook until golden brown each side.

- Serve hot.

Variation

- If the batter is made very runny, very thin pancakes can be made that cover the base of the pan. These should be sprinkled with lemon juice and rolled up, before serving hot.

Buckwheat Pancakes

Makes 12–16 pancakes
4 oz/100 g buckwheat flour
4 oz/100 g wholemeal flour
salt to taste
1 teaspoon baking powder
1 tablespoon olive oil
2 eggs
½ pint/300 ml water

- Mix the flours, salt, baking powder and olive oil together.

- Mix the eggs into the flour mixture and add enough water to form a thin and runny batter.

- Heat a heavy-based frying pan.

- Drop the batter into the pan in spoonfuls and immediately spread as thinly as possible. Cook until brown each side.

- Serve hot with lemon juice.

Scots Pancakes

Makes 12–16 pancakes
4 oz/100 g plain flour
4 oz/100 g wholemeal flour
salt to taste
1 teaspoon baking powder
1 oz/25 g lard or butter
2 eggs
½ pint/300 ml water

- Mix the flours, salt, naking powder and lard/butter together.

- Mix the eggs into the flour mixture and add enough water to form a thick pouring batter.

- Heat a heavy-based frying pan, to a moderate heat only.

- Drop the batter into the pan in spoonfuls, and cook until golden brown each side. Turn as soon as the bubbles in the middle start to break.

- Serve hot with butter.

Doughnuts

It is important that deep-frying fat is hot, otherwise the dough will absorb too much fat and become soggy. Take care with hot fat. Use a large pan with a small amount of oil and always have a close-fitting lid available for the pan, in case of fire, and never leave hot fat unattended.

Makes 24 doughnuts
1 oz/25 g fresh yeast or 1 tablespoon dried yeast +1 teaspoon sugar
½ pint/300 ml warm water
8 oz/225 g wholemeal flour
8 oz/225 g white flour
2 oz/50 g butter
salt to taste

- Crumble the fresh yeast into the water or mix in the dried yeast and sugar. Keep warm until the yeast is working well.

- Mix the flours and salt together. Then rub the butter into the mixture.

- Slowly mix the flour into the liquid until a uniform soft dough is formed. Don't knead.

- Cover with an oiled polythene sheet and leave in a warm place for 1 hour, when it should double in bulk.

- Use floured hands to shape the dough into balls 1½ inches/4 cm in diameter. Place on a floured board.

- Cover the dough with an oiled polythene sheet and keep warm until the dough has risen again.

- Heat the frying oil in a large pan to 375°F, 190°C.

- Deep-fry the balls of dough a few at a time for 10 minutes, until golden brown.

- Stand the doughnuts on kitchen paper to drain off surplus fat.

- Serve hot.

Variation

- Add 1 teaspoon of mixed spice to the flour mixture.

Starch Crispbreads and Crackers

Oatcakes

Makes 12 oatcakes
8 oz/225 g medium oatmeal
1 tablespoon molasses
1 oz/25 g melted lard
salt to taste
boiling water

- Mix all the ingredients together with enough boiling water to make a soft dough.

- Knead well, and roll out thinly on a floured board.

- Cut the dough into rounds and place the crispbreads on a greased tray.

- Bake in a preheated oven, gas mark 6, 400°F, 200°C, for 8–12 minutes until brown

- Turn out onto a wire tray to cool and dry.

- Keep oatcakes in an airtight container.

Variation

- Use wholemeal flour in place of half the oatmeal.

Corn Crisps

Makes 20 corn crisps
8 oz/225 g cornmeal
salt to taste
½ pint/300 ml boiling water
2 tablespoons corn oil

- Mix the cornmeal and salt together.

- The water should be on the boil as the mixture is stirred in to make a thick batter. If it is too solid, add more boiling water. Stand for five minutes and then stir in the oil.

- Place spoonfuls of the batter on a well-greased baking tray and spread out into 3 inch/7.5 cm rounds.

- Bake in a preheated oven, gas mark 6, 400°F, 200°C, for 15 minutes until golden brown.

- Serve hot.

Variation

- Corn pones are thicker. Spoon 2 tablespoons of batter for each pone onto the baking tray and don't spread them out. They should be brown round the edges when cooked.

Millet and Sesame Crispbread

Makes 12–20 small crispbreads
4 oz/100 g sesame seed
4 oz/100 g millet grain
1 oz/25 g melted lard
2½ fl oz/65 ml boiling water
salt to taste

- Mix the whole seed and grain together and then grind them into a flour with a grain mill or coffee mill. Add salt. A pestle and mortar works best, but it is hard work!

- Mix in the melted lard.

- Add boiling water until the mixture forms a soft dough.

- Spread over a greased tray and press down very firmly to a thickness of ⅛ inch/3 mm. Score into squares.

- Bake in a preheated oven, gas mark 6, 400°F, 200°C, for 8–12 minutes until golden brown.

- Turn out onto a wire tray to cool and dry.

- Keep crispbreads in an airtight container.

Variations

- Use cornmeal or ground rice in place of the millet grain.

Sunflower Crispbread

Makes 12–15 small crispbreads
4 oz/100 g sunflower seeds
4 oz/100 g sweet-chestnut purée
salt to taste
1 oz/25 g melted lard
2 oz/50 g ground rice

- Liquidize the sunflower seeds with the sweet-chestnut purée. Add salt.

- Mix in the melted lard.

- Mix in the ground rice.

- Roll out a walnut-sized lump of dough between two sheets of silicone-coated or greaseproof paper until it is less than ⅛ inch/3 mm thick.

- Place the crispbreads on a greased tray.

- Bake in a preheated oven, gas mark 6, 400°F, 200°C, for 8–12 minutes until golden brown.

- Turn out onto a wire tray to cool and dry.

- Keep crispbreads in an airtight container.

Rye Crispbread

Makes 15 small crispbreads
½ oz/15 g fresh yeast or ½ tablespoon dried yeast +1 teaspoon sugar
½ pint/300 ml warm water
4 oz/100 g rye flour
4 oz/100 g wholemeal flour
1 oz/25 g cornmeal
salt to taste
1 tablespoon molasses
1 tablespoon olive oil

- Crumble the fresh yeast into the water or mix in the dried yeast and sugar. Keep warm until the yeast is working well.

- Mix all the dry ingredients together. Then mix in the molasses and oil.

- Slowly mix the flour into the liquid until a uniform dough is formed.

- Knead for 10–15 minutes into a smooth dough.

- Leave in a warm place for 1 hour, when it should double in bulk.

- Roll out thinly and cut into squares.

- Place the crispbreads on a greased tray and leave to rise again for 1 hour.

- Bake in a preheated oven, gas mark 6, 400°F, 200°C, for 8–12 minutes until golden brown.

- Turn out onto a wire tray to cool and dry.

- Keep crispbreads in an airtight container.

Starch Cakes without Sugar or Protein

Fruity Malt Bread

Makes two 1 lb/450 g loaves
8 fl oz/250 ml warm water
1 oz/25 g butter, softened
2 tablespoons malt extract
1 tablespoon black treacle or molasses
1 oz/25 g fresh yeast or 1 tablespoon dried yeast +1 teaspoon castor
  sugar
1 lb/450 g wholemeal flour
5 oz/150 g sultanas
1 oz/25 g peel

- Pour the water into a bowl and add the butter, malt extract, treacle/molasses and yeast. Mix thoroughly.

- Add the flour and fruit and mix again.

- Turn onto a floured board and knead until the dough is smooth and elastic.

- Shape into two loaves and put in two greased 1 lb/450 g loaf tins.

- Cover with a clean cloth and put into a warm place until doubled in size.

- Bake at gas mark 6, 400°F, 200°C, for 35–45 minutes.

- Turn out and cool on a wire rack.

Variations

- Chopped dates or chopped dried apricots may be used in place of the fruit, or chopped nuts in place of the peel.

- Honey may be used in place of the treacle.

Stollen

Makes 2 1 lb/450 g cake
1 oz/25 g fresh yeast or 1 tablespoon dried yeast +1 teaspoon sugar
3 fl oz/85 ml warm water
1 oz/25 g butter, softened
1 tablespoon black treacle or molasses
8 oz/225 g wholemeal flour
1 oz/25 g sultanas
1 oz/25 g glacé cherries, chopped
1 oz/25 g dates, chopped
1 oz/25 g peel
1 egg, beaten
grated rind of 1 lemon

- Crumble the fresh yeast into the water or mix in the dried yeast and sugar. Keep warm until the yeast is working well.
- Rub the butter and treacle molasses into the flour.
- Mix in the dried fruit. Then add the beaten egg and lemon rind.
- Slowly mix the flour into the liquid until a uniform soft dough is formed.
- Turn onto a floured board and knead until the dough is smooth and elastic.
- Shape into two loaves and put into two greased 1 lb/450 g loaf tins.
- Cover with a clean cloth and put in a warm place until doubled in size.
- Re-knead the dough and shape into 2 oblongs 10 × 8 inches/ 25 × 20 cm.
- Fold the dough in half, gently, and place each loaf on a greased baking tray.
- Bake at gas mark 5, 375°F, 190°C, for 25–30 minutes.
- Turn out and cool on a wire rack.

Variations

- Chopped dried apricots and figs may be used in place of the fruit.
- Add 1 ground clove or 1 teaspoon of mixed spice to the flour.

Apple Gingerbread

Makes one 1 lb/450 g cake
8 oz/225 g wholemeal flour
2 teaspoons raising agent
1 teaspoon ginger
1 teaspoon mixed spice
1 oz/25 g butter, softened
1 tablespoon olive oil
1 large cooking apple
5 oz/150 g sultanas
1 tablespoon black treacle or molasses
¼ pint/150 ml water
salt to taste

- Mix the flour, raising agent, ginger and spice thoroughly.

- Rub in the butter and oil.

- Peel and grate the apple coarsely. Add the fruit and the treacle/molasses, then mix again.

- Mix with a little water to a soft, but not sticky, dough. Do not use all the water if it is not needed!

- Roll out to about an 8 inch/20 cm round. Place on a greased baking tray.

- Bake at gas mark 6, 400°F, 200°C, for 25–30 minutes.

- Turn out and cool on a wire rack.

Variations

- Chopped dates or chopped dried apricots may be used in place of the fruit.

- Honey may be used in place of the treacle.

Parkin

Makes one 1 lb/450 g cake
2 oz/50 g butter
6 oz/175 g wholemeal flour
3 oz/75 g molasses
1 teaspoon ground ginger
2 oz/50 g dates, chopped
2 oz/50 g figs, chopped
2 oz/50 g medium oatmeal
1 egg, beaten
2 fl oz/50 ml milk
salt to taste

- Rub the butter into the flour.

- Mix in the molasses, ginger and fruit.

- Mix in the oatmeal and the egg.

- Mix in enough milk to form a stiff batter.

- Pour into a greased and lined bread tin.

- Bake in a preheated oven, gas mark 5, 375°F, 190°C for 1½ hours, or until done (check with a skewer – see page 94).

- Turn out to cool on a wire rack.

Pumpkin and Spice Bread

Makes one 1 lb/450 g cake
8 oz/225 g wholemeal flour
2 oz/50 g ground almonds
salt to taste
2 teaspoons raising agent
1½ teaspoons ground cinnamon
½ teaspoon nutmeg
1 teaspoon mixed spice
1 oz/25 g butter, softened
1 tablespoon olive oil
6 oz/175 g pumpkin purée or courgette purée
1 tablespoon honey
2 tablespoons black treacle or molasses
¼ pint/150 ml water

- Mix the flour, almonds, raising agent and spices thoroughly.

- Rub in the butter and oil.

- Mix in the pumpkin or courgette purée, honey, and the treacle/molasses.

- Mix with a little water to a soft, but not sticky, dough. Do not use all the water if it is not needed!

- Roll out to about an 8 inch/20 cm round. Place on a greased baking tray.

- Bake at gas mark 6, 400°F, 200°C, for 25–30 minutes.

- Cool for 10 minutes before turning out and cooling on a wire rack.

Apple and Fruit Slice

Makes 2 lb/900 g
1 lb/450 g eating apples, chopped
3 oz/75 g hazelnuts, chopped
4 oz/100 g dates, chopped
½ teaspoon ground cinnamon
½ teaspoon nutmeg
1 oz/25 g butter, softened
1 tablespoon olive oil
1 tablespoon honey
2 tablespoons black treacle or molasses
1 egg, beaten
4 oz/100 g flaked oats or flaked rice

- Mix all the ingredients together.

- Line a shallow 11 × 8 inch/28 × 20 cm tin with foil.

- Spread the mixed ingredients over the foil.

- Bake at gas mark 4, 350°F, 180°C, for 25–30 minutes.

- Allow to go cold before cutting into fingers and turning out of the tin.

Variations

- Pumpkin slice: use 1 lb/450 g of chopped pumpkin flesh in place of the apple.

- Chopped figs or chopped dried apricots may be used in place of the dates.

- Chocolate may be used in place of the butter.

Cereal Bar

Makes 1½ lb/680 g
3 oz/75 g butter
1 tablespoon honey
2 tablespoons black treacle or molasses
4 oz/100 g cornflakes
4 oz/100 g oat flakes
4 oz/100 g flaked rice
3 oz/75 g hazelnuts, chopped
3 oz/75 g dates, chopped

- Melt the butter, honey and black treacle/molasses together over a gentle heat.

- Stir in the cornflakes, oat flakes and flaked rice, together with the nuts and dates and ensure that they are well mixed.

- Line a shallow 11 × 8 inch/28 × 20 cm tin with foil.

- Spread the mixed ingredients over the foil and press down well.

- Bake at gas mark 2, 300°F, 150°C for 30–45 minutes.

- Cut into fingers while hot and then leave to cool in the tin.

Variations

- Sultanas, chopped figs or chopped dried apricots may be used in place of the dates.

Starch Breakfasts

Muesli

Makes 1 lb/450 g
2 oz/50 g oat flakes
2 oz/50 g flaked rice
2 oz/50 g hazelnuts, chopped
2 oz/50 g dates, chopped
2 oz/50 g figs, chopped
2 oz/50 g banana chips
2 oz/50 g honey or black treacle or molasses
2 oz/50 g shredded coconut

- Mix all the ingredients together.

- Use as required. You can keep the mixture in a sealed container in a cool, dry place for up to week.

- Serve with fruit juice (mix the fruit juice with the muesli).

Variations

- Sultanas, raisins or chopped dried apricots may be used in place of the dates.

Oatmeal Porridge

The best porridge is made by simmering medium-ground oatmeal overnight beside a peat fire. The quickest is made from oat flakes in a microwave.

Overnight method

Per person
2 oz/50 g medium ground oatmeal
¼ pint/150 ml water
salt to taste

- Soak the oatmeal in the water overnight.

- In the morning, simmer gently for 35–40 minutes until the porridge is soft and smooth.

- Salt to taste after cooking.

- Serve with a small amount of cream (no sugar).

Microwave method

Per person
2 oz/50 g flaked oats
¼ pint/150 ml water
salt to taste

- Place the oats and water in your microwave bowl. The water should just cover the oats.

- Microwave at a simmer for 4 minutes.

- Salt to taste after cooking.

- Serve with a small amount of cream (no sugar).

Millet and Date Porridge

Per person
2 oz/50 g millet grain
2 oz/50 g dates, chopped
¼ pint/150 ml water

- Soak the millet and dates in the water overnight.

- In the morning, simmer gently for 35–40 minutes until the millet is tender but nutty.

- Serve with fruit juice.

Variations

- Sultanas, raisins or chopped dried apricots may be used in place of the dates.

Rice and Sultanas

Per person
2 oz/50 g brown rice
2 oz/50 g sultanas
¼ pint/150 ml water

- Soak the rice and sultanas in the water overnight.

- In the morning, simmer gently for 35–40 minutes until the rice is tender but nutty.

- Serve with fruit juice.

Variations

- Pre-cooked brown rice reduces the cooking time to 20 minutes.

- Dates, raisins or chopped dried apricots may be used in place of the sultanas.

Polenta

Per person
2 oz/50 g maize cornmeal – often sold as polenta
½ oz/15 g butter
¼ pint/150 ml water
cream to taste
salt to taste

- Mix the polenta with the butter and water while cold and then bring slowly to the boil in a heavy-bottomed pan.

- Stir it frequently as the polenta thickens, for 30 minutes.

- Serve with a little cream.

Variations

- Pour the cooked polenta into a greased tray to set. Allow to cool and cut into squares. Fry the squares in olive oil and serve hot.

Kasha

This strongly flavoured breakfast dish originates in Eastern Europe.

Per person
2 oz/50 g buckwheat grain or flake
¼ pint/150 ml water
½ oz/15 g butter
salt and cream or honey to taste

- Roast the grain dry in a heavy-bottomed pan to develop the flavour.

- Soak the grain in the water overnight.

- Add the butter and salt and simmer over the lowest possible heat for 3 hours, adding more water if required. Traditionally this dish was simmered beside the ashes of the fire overnight.

- Serve with a little cream or honey.

Quinnoa

This grain is quick to cook and nourishing, but it must be well washed in boiling water first, to remove all traces of a bitter flavour.

Per person
2 oz/50 g quinnoa grain
1 kettle and ¼ pint/150 ml water
cream or honey and salt to taste

- Place the quinnoa grain in a fine sieve and rinse it with a kettle of boiling water.

- Simmer the grain in the water for 15 minutes and then drain.

- Serve with a little cream or honey.

Starch Main Meals

Pasta

Pasta should always be cooked just before serving. Dry pasta should be added to a large pan of boiling water, salted to taste. Allow 2 pints of water per 4 oz pasta or 1 litres of water per 100 g pasta.

Different thicknesses and shapes of pasta require slightly different cooking times, so check the manufacturer's instructions and test the pasta 2 minutes and 1 minute before the cooking time is up. It should be firm to the bite, but not hard. If overcooked it will become a soft and sticky mass.

Drain the pasta and then return to the pan. Toss the cooked pasta with a little olive oil, enough to separate the strands, then toss again with the chosen sauce and serve immediately.

Long, thin, round pasta, such as spaghetti and vermicelli, is traditionally served with a thin, olive oil-based sauce. Long, flat pasta, such as tagliatelle, is served with thicker and richer sauces, and short, tubular pasta needs a thinner sauce that will flow into the tubes.

The starch and pesto sauces on pages 153–4 and 210 respectively can be served with pasta, or can be used as dips with crudités, served on bread or as a filling for sandwiches.

Baked Potato

Very large potatoes can be difficult to cook, and they are more likely to be blackened inside. Select unblemished, medium-sized potatoes if possible.

Per person
2 or 3 medium-sized potatoes make a reasonable meal
olive oil

- Scrub the potatoes and dry them.

- Prick them a few times with a fork.

- Wipe them with olive oil.

- Bake in a preheated oven, gas mark 5, 375°F, 190°C, until soft.

- Baking time does depend on the size of the potato, from 40 minutes for small potatoes to 80 minutes for larger ones.

- Serve with a little olive oil or butter, and a salad or a selection of vegetables.

Baked Sweet Potato

Sweet potatoes bake to a soft and sweet pulp.

Per person
1 large sweet potato

- Scrub the potato clean.

- Bake in a preheated oven, gas mark 5, 375°F, 190°C, until soft.

- Baking time does depend on the size of the potato, from 30 minutes for small potatoes to 60 minutes for larger ones.

- Serve with a little olive oil or butter, and a salad or a selection of vegetables.

Potato Pizza

Per person
Leftover mashed potato, enough to make a 6 inch/15 cm round
knob of butter
olive oil
1 medium onion, finely chopped
2 oz/50 g mushrooms, chopped or sliced
hot water
1 clove garlic, crushed
1 tomato
fresh herbs to taste

- Make a 6 inch/15 cm round of mashed potato for each person and spread with a little butter.

- Put it into the oven or under the grill to heat through.

- Heat the olive oil in a pan and fry the onion, mushrooms and garlic gently until cooked.

- Add a little hot water and simmer until you have a thick sauce.

- Spread this sauce on the potato, top with a sliced tomato and sprinkle the herbs on top.

- Replace under the grill until the tomatoes are *lightly* cooked.

- Serve with a salad.

- If you do not wish to cook the tomatoes at all, they can be served fresh with the salad.

Variations

- Add chopped nuts and sesame seeds to the onion and mushrooms.

- Add bean sprouts to the onion and mushrooms.

Potato Roast

Roast potatoes often contain too much fat, and the food combining diets avoids eating roast potatoes with the roast meat. Here is an excellent way of roasting potatoes without the meat!

Per person
2 or 3 medium-sized potatoes
olive oil

- Scrub and dry the potatoes – there is no need to peel them. Most of the nutrients lie immediately below the skin.

- Cut the potatoes into quarters, boil in water for 5–10 minutes, until just softening on the outside, then drain.

- Brush the potatoes with olive oil.

- Bake in a preheated oven, gas mark 5, 375°F, 190°C, for 1 hour: after 30 minutes and again after 45 minutes brush the potatoes with olive oil.

- Serve with a wine sauce (see page 154) and a selection of vegetables.

Potato Crisps (Pakoras)

It is important that deep-frying fat is hot, otherwise the dough will absorb too much fat and become soggy. Take care with hot fat. Use a large pan with a small amount of oil and always have a close-fitting lid available for the pan, in case of fire, and never leave hot fat unattended.

Makes 1½ lb/680 g of crisps
8 oz/225 g chickpea flour or gram flour
salt to taste
2 teaspoons ground sesame seeds
1 teaspoon ground coriander
1 teaspoon ground cumin
½ teaspoon chilli powder
1 lb/450 g potatoes, sliced as thinly as possible
7 fl oz/200 ml water as required – you may not need it all
deep-frying oil

- Mix the flour, salt, sesame seeds and spices in a large bowl.

- Add the sliced potato and mix well.

- Add a little water as you mix, until the potato slices are covered with a thick paste.

- Heat the cooking oil, but do not let it get so hot that it produces smoke.

- Add the potato slices, a few at a time. If you add too many the temperature will drop and they will stick together.

- Fry the crisps for 6 minutes or until golden brown.

- Drain on absorbent paper. Serve hot or cold.

Variation

- Sweetcorn pakoras can also be made using sweetcorn in place of the potato and using maize flour.

Spicy Potatoes

Serves 4
1 lb/450 g new potatoes, or old potatoes, cut into chunks
4 tablespoons olive oil
1 teaspoon chilli powder
1 teaspoon paprika
1 teaspoon ground coriander
juice of 1 lime or lemon
1 teaspoon sugar
salt
1 tablespoon chopped fresh basil
1 tablespoon chopped fresh coriander

- Sauté the potatoes in the oil for 5 minutes until golden all over.

- Add the spices, lime/lemon juice, sugar and salt.

- Cover and cook for 10–15 more minutes, until the potatoes are tender.

- Sprinkle with the chopped herbs, toss and serve.

Hot Garlic Potatoes

Serves 4

1 onion, chopped
2 cloves garlic, peeled and crushed
4 tablespoons olive oil
1 teaspoon turmeric
2 green chillies, finely chopped
1 lb/450 g new potatoes (small potatoes can be left whole but larger
  potatoes should be sliced)
8 oz/225 g tomatoes, skinned and chopped
3 oz/75 g sultanas
salt
1 small carton cream
2 oz/50 g toasted pine kernels
2 tablespoons fresh coriander, chopped

- Fry the onion and garlic in the oil until soft.

- Add the turmeric and chillies and fry for a further 2 minutes.

- Add the potatoes, stir and cover. Cook for about 5 minutes,
  stirring several times.

- Add the tomatoes, sultanas and salt. Cook uncovered for a
  few minutes.

- Fry gently until the potatoes are cooked.

- Toss the potato mixture in the cream.

- Sprinkle with pine kernels and coriander, and serve hot.

Cretan Shepherd's Pie

Serves 4
2 onions, sliced
2 cloves garlic, chopped or crushed
1 lb/450 g courgettes, sliced
3 tablespoons olive oil
6 large tomatoes, skinned and chopped
1 tablespoon tomato purée
salt and pepper
1 tablespoon chopped fresh basil
1½ lb/680 g boiled, mashed potato

- Fry the onions, garlic and courgettes in the oil until soft.

- Add the tomatoes, tomato purée and seasoning. Simmer for 5 minutes.

- Add the basil, then turn into an oven dish and cover with the mashed potato.

- Cook in the oven at gas mark 6, 400°F, 200°C, for 30 minutes until golden.

- Serve with a salad.

Rice Dishes

- Always take the time to rinse the grains of rice well in cold water and to check the rice for grit.

- Allow 2 oz/50 g of rice per person for a main meal.

- Add twice the volume of water to the volume of rice.

- Bring the water to a good rolling boil for 3 minutes.

- Cover the pan tightly and reduce the heat to the lowest possible simmer for 40 minutes to 1 hour. Most of the water will be absorbed by the rice and it should not be stirred while cooking.

- Remove from the heat and allow to stand for 5 minutes before serving.

- Cooking brown rice in a pressure cooker reduces the cooking time to 35–45 minutes.

- Parboiled brown rice needs to be simmered for 25–30 minutes.

- The best way to reheat cooked rice is by steaming for 15 minutes.

Popped rice

- Cover the uncooked rice with cold water.

- Change the water morning and night until the rice has soaked for 3 full 24-hour days.

- Drain the rice and heat it in a heavy-bottomed frying pan, stirring constantly until all the rice has turned brown and popped.

- Popped rice can be stored for several weeks in an airtight container.

- It makes a crunchy addition to muesli, or for a snack.

Fried rice

- For each 2 oz/50 g portion, heat 1 tablespoon of olive oil in a deep frying pan until the oil is smoking. Then stir in the rice.

- Fry over a moderate heat for 5 minutes. White rice will turn a translucent white again, but this change is not so easy to see in brown rice.

- Add 7 fl oz/200 ml water or vegetable stock for each 2 oz/50 g portion and simmer over the lowest heat until tender.

- The frying oil can be flavoured with cumin seeds, cassia, cloves and black peppercorns. These should be fried for 30 seconds before the rice is added.

Rice with a Hot Vegetable Sauce

Per person
2 oz/50 g rice
olive oil
1 medium onion
4 oz/100 g mushrooms
boiling water
herbs as available (thyme, sage, rosemary, etc.)
1 green vegetable as available (chopped courgettes, broccoli, shredded
    cabbage, bean sprouts, banana plantain, carrot, swede, etc.)

- Start by cooking the rice, either in a saucepan or microwave oven.

- While this is cooking, cover the bottom of a frying pan thinly with olive oil and heat through.

- Chop the onion and drop it into the oil, frying gently until it is beginning to turn transparent.

- Chop the mushrooms and add to the onion.

- Fry together until the onion is golden brown and the mushroom softened.

- Now cover with just enough boiling water to prevent the onion and mushroom from burning, and simmer.

- Towards the end of the cooking time, add the herbs and green vegetable and cover with a lid, to simmer until the rice and vegetables are ready.

- Serve the sauce on a bed of rice.

Variations

- Add pine kernels or chopped nuts with the green vegetable.

- Sprinkle sesame seeds on top.

- Add garlic towards the end of the cooking period.

- Use a little soya sauce for added flavour.

Cashew Nut Pilaf

Pilaf is a national dish from Turkey, cooked in the oven. It is important that the rice is not stirred while cooking.

Serves 4
8 oz/225 g long-grain rice
1 oz/25 g each cashew nuts, pine kernels – or any variation
1 oz/25 g each sultanas, raisins, hazelnuts, walnuts
4 oz/100 g dried figs, chopped
4 oz/100 g mushrooms
1 small to medium onion, chopped
1 clove garlic, crushed
herbs (rosemary, thyme, oregano)
salt to taste
4–6 fl oz/120–175 ml boiling water

The pilaf may be baked in the oven or in a microwave oven.

Oven method

- Mix all the ingredients together in an ovenproof dish and bring to the boil.

- Place in a low oven (gas mark 2, 300°F, 150°C), and simmer gently for 45 minutes.

Microwave method

- Mix all the ingredients together in a large microwave-proof bowl.

- Cover with clingfilm and pierce several times.

- Cook at full power for 20 minutes.

- The rice should absorb all the water when fully cooked, and the pilaf can be served straight from the bowl.

Persian-Style Rice

Serves 4
8 oz/225 g basmati rice
1 oz/25 g butter
1 bay leaf
1 oz/25 g cashew nuts
1 oz/25 g flaked almonds
1 oz/25 g sultanas
½ oz/15 g grated coconut
½ teaspoon poppy seed
½ teaspoon fennel seed
¾ pint/450 ml boiling water
salt to taste

- Cover the basmati rice with cold water and soak for 1 hour, then drain.

- Heat the butter in a heavy-bottomed saucepan, then fry the bay leaf briefly.

- Add the drained rice to the saucepan and stir in all the other ingredients except for the water and salt.

- When well mixed, add the boiling water, and bring the contents of the pan back to a rolling boil for 3 minutes.

- Reduce the heat to a simmer until the rice is cooked and all the water absorbed – check every few minutes, it doesn't take very long.

- Serve with a range of vegetables and a curry sauce.

Nutty-Flavoured Risotto

Risotto involves cooking the rice, vegetables and flavourings together in a pan over the heat. Traditionally short-grained rice is used for this dish.

Serves 4
1 pint/600 ml vegetable stock
1 small onion, finely chopped
1 tablespoon olive oil
8 oz/225 g short-grain rice
1 oz/25 g cashew nuts or peanuts
1 oz/25 g flaked almonds
1 oz/25 g hazelnuts, chopped
1 oz/25 g Brazil nuts or sesame seeds, chopped
1 oz/25 g butter
salt to taste

- Heat the vegetable stock in a separate pan and keep it simmering.

- In a heavy-bottomed saucepan, fry the onion in the olive oil until soft, then add the rice and fry gently for 1 minute, stirring well.

- Slowly add one-third of the stock to the rice and simmer, stirring, for 5 minutes until all the liquid is absorbed.

- Add the next third of stock and continue to stir, simmering for 10–12 minutes until it is also absorbed.

- Add the chopped nuts and the remaining third of stock and continue to simmer for 20 minutes while the rice thickens. Add more liquid if required.

- Remove from the heat and stir in the butter and salt before serving.

Stuffed Vine or Cabbage Leaves

Serves 4
8 large vine or cabbage leaves
1 onion, chopped
1 tablespoon olive oil
4 oz/100 g long-grain brown rice
1 oz/25 g sultanas
1 oz/25 g dried apricots, chopped
3 oz/75 g nuts, chopped (hazelnut, almond, Brazil, walnut, pecan, cashew)
1 tablespoon chopped parsley
1 tablespoon chopped basil, marjoram or oregano
salt and pepper to taste
1 can chopped tomatoes
¼ pint/150 ml water

- Drop the vine or cabbage leaves into boiling water for 2 minutes, then set aside.

- Cook the onion gently in the oil for 2–3 minutes.

- Stir in the rice, sultanas, apricot, nuts and herbs. Season and mix well.

- Spread each vine or cabbage leaf on a plate and place an equal portion of the mixture on each leaf. Roll up into parcels, tucking in the ends. Place in a large saucepan, joined sides down.

- Mix the tomatoes and water and pour over the leaves.

- Simmer gently for at least an hour.

- Remove the parcels from the pan when cooked and place them on a dish to keep warm.

- If necessary, boil the remaining liquid to reduce it to a sauce.

- Pour the tomato mixture over the leaves and serve.

Millet and Nut Pilaf

Allow 2 oz/50 g of millet per person. Millet is best soaked for at least 1 hour in cold water before use. It should be placed in twice its own volume of water, brought to the boil and then simmered gently for 40 minutes. Millet keeps a firmer texture than rice. The larger green-grained millets have a better texture than the smaller yellow-grained millets.

Serves 4
8 oz/225 g millet
1 oz/25 g butter
1 small onion, finely chopped
2 tablespoons olive oil
4 oz/100 g mixed nuts chopped (cashew nuts, peanuts, pine nuts, flaked almonds, hazelnuts, Brazil nuts or sesame seeds)
fresh herbs, chopped
soya sauce to taste
salt to taste
1 pint/600 ml vegetable stock

- Mix all the ingredients together in a heavy-based pan with a tight-fitting lid.

- Bring to the boil and then simmer on the lowest heat for 40 minutes.

Samosas

Makes 18 samosas
For the pastry:
8 oz/225 g plain flour
8 oz/225 g wholemeal flour
2 tablespoons olive oil
salt to taste
4 fl oz/120 ml warm water
For the filling:
1 teaspoon cumin seeds
1 oz/25 g sesame seeds
1 medium onion, finely chopped
5 tablespoons olive oil
¼ teaspoon chilli powder
salt to taste
¼ teaspoon turmeric
12 oz/350 g potatoes, cut into small cubes
6 oz/175 g green peas
1 large carrot, grated
juice of ½ lemon
2 teaspoons garam masala
2 teaspoons molasses
1 tablespoon chopped coriander leaves
oil for deep frying

- Mix all the pastry ingredients together and knead to form a firm dough. Leave for 30 minutes.

- Fry the cumin, sesame seeds and the onion in the oil for 5 minutes.

- Add the chilli, salt and turmeric, followed by the potatoes, and mix well.

- Cook over a low heat for 10 minutes, stirring occasionally, then add the peas and carrot and keep over a low heat until cooked.

- The lemon juice, garam masala and molasses should be mixed in well and cooked for a further 2 minutes before the coriander is added.

- Allow the mixture to cool before filling the samosas.

- Divide the dough into 18 balls. Roll out each ball on a floured surface to about 6 inches/15 cm in diameter, then fold each in half.

- Put a tablespoonful of mixture in the middle of each samosa, then fold over again and seal firmly. It helps if you moisten the edges.

- Heat the frying oil in a large pan, using a fat thermometer to check that the temperature is close to 350°F, 180°C.

- Fry the samosas until golden brown.

- Drain on absorbent paper.

- Serve hot.

Pasta Salads

Pasta salads are best made with eggless short pasta, such as macaroni and rigatoni. The pasta should not be overcooked or it will lose its texture. It should be rinsed with hot water, while the pasta is still hot, and tossed in the dressing while still warm.

The dressing may be simply olive oil and lemon juice, or may be combined with the fresh herbs of a pesto.

Pasta salad can be served with other salad vegetables, cooked or raw, and a selection of fresh herbs.

Pasta with Pesto Salad

Serves 4
8 oz/225 g macaroni
4 pints/2 litres water
2 oz/50 g basil leaves, washed and dried
2 oz/50 g garlic cloves, peeled and crushed
2 oz/50 g pine nuts
4 tablespoons olive oil

- Add the dry pasta to a large pan of boiling water, salted to taste.

- Different thicknesses and shapes of pasta require slightly different cooking times, so check the manufacturers' instructions and test the pasta 2 minutes and 1 minute before the cooking time is up. It should be firm to the bite, but not hard. If overcooked it will become a soft and sticky mass.

- Drain the pasta then rinse with a kettle of boiling water and drain again.

- Return the pasta to the pan.

- Liquidize the basil, garlic and pine nuts with half the olive oil, then beat in the remaining oil much more gently.

- Toss the warm pasta with the pesto and allow to cool before serving.

Rice Salad

Serves 4
3 tablespoons olive oil
3 tablespoons lemon juice
2 tablespoons chopped parsley
salt to taste
selection of vegetables – enough to fill a ½ pint/300 ml measure:
  beans, cooked
  avocado, cut into small cubes
  carrot, shredded, raw
  peas, raw if garden fresh, otherwise cooked
  celery, diced
  cauliflower, raw, diced
  courgettes, sliced thinly, raw if garden fresh, otherwise cooked
  radish
  tomato, raw, sliced
  olives
  garlic, finely chopped
8 oz/225 g wholegrain brown rice, cooked

- Mix the first four ingredients to make a marinade.

- Mix all the selected ingredients together.

- Rest in the marinade for 1 hour before serving with the rice.

- This salad can be kept in the refrigerator for up to 1 day.

Starch Soups

Vegetable Stock

A good stock forms the basis for a good soup. Stock cubes are often based on protein, and should be used only for protein soups.

Makes 1 pint/600 ml stock
2 pints/1 litre water
1 onion, sliced
1 carrot
1 bay leaf
4 black peppercorns, whole
salt to taste
1 oz/25 g mung beans or lentils
1 small potato, chopped

- Place all the ingredients together in a pressure cooker, and cook under high pressure for 45 minutes: without a pressure cooker, bring to the boil, then simmer gently for 1½ hours.

- Remove the bay leaf and peppercorns.

- Liquidize the stock.

- Simmer in an open pan to reduce the volume to 1 pint/600 ml.

- Freeze the stock in small quantities, if required, for later use.

Cauliflower and Potato Soup

Serves 4
½ cauliflower
1 medium onion, finely chopped
2 medium potatoes, diced as small as possible
½ teaspoon thyme leaves
fresh ground pepper to taste
salt to taste
1 pint/600 ml vegetable stock

- Cook the cauliflower, onion and potato, and herbs and seasoning, in the stock until soft.

- Liquidize all the vegetables in the stock.

- Serve with any fresh bread.

Bean Soup

Serves 4
1 oz/25 g mung beans
1 oz/25 g azuki beans
1 oz/25 g blackeye beans
1 pint/600 ml vegetable stock
1 oz/25 g yellow split peas
fresh ground black pepper to taste
¼ teaspoon ground turmeric
1 powdered clove

- Soak the beans in 1 pint/600 ml water overnight. Discard the water and rinse the beans.

- Place all the ingredients together in a large saucepan and bring to the boil.

- Simmer for 1½ hours.

- Serve with any fresh bread.

149

Scotch Broth

Serves 4
1 medium onion
1 medium leek
1 large carrot
½ swede
2 medium potatoes
2 oz/50 g barley or rice
salt to taste
1 pint/600 ml vegetable stock

- Dice all the vegetables as finely as possible – do not liquidize.
- Add all the ingredients to the stock.
- Bring to the boil and simmer for 1 hour.
- Serve with any fresh bread.

Mushroom and Watercress Soup

Serves 4
1 medium onion, finely chopped
2 cloves garlic, crushed
2 tablespoons olive oil
1 oz/25 g cornflour
1 pint/600 ml vegetable stock
8 oz/225 mushrooms, thinly sliced
2 tablespoons watercress, chopped
salt to taste

- Fry the onion and garlic gently in the oil for 5 minutes.
- Mix the cornflour to a paste with a little *cold* water, then whisk into the stock.
- Add the onion and garlic to the stock and bring to the boil, stirring continuously as the soup thickens.
- Add the mushrooms and watercress to the soup and simmer for a further 5 minutes.
- Season and serve with any fresh bread.

Beetroot Soup

Serves 4
8 oz/225 g beetroot, chopped
4 oz/100 g carrot, chopped
4 oz/100 g onion, chopped
2 cloves garlic, crushed
2 tablespoons olive oil
1 pint/600 ml vegetable stock
salt to taste

- Fry all the vegetables gently in the oil for 5 minutes.

- Add them to the stock and bring to the boil.

- Simmer gently for 40 minutes.

- Allow to cool slightly, then liquidize.

- Season and serve with any fresh bread.

Starch Sauces

Velouté Sauce

Velouté sauces, made from a mixture of flour and butter, are rich and creamy and can be served with any starch-based meal, but in moderation only.

Makes ½ pint/300 ml sauce
1 oz/25 g butter
1 oz/25 g flour
¾ pint/450 ml vegetable stock (boiling)
2 fl oz/50 ml cream (optional)
salt to taste
white pepper to taste

- Melt the butter in a heavy-bottomed saucepan.

- Beat the flour into the melted butter and cook over a low heat for 2 minutes. The butter should not go darker than a straw colour.

- Remove the pan from the heat and allow to cool slightly before stirring in the boiling stock, a little at a time.

- Bring the sauce back to the boil and continue to stir as the sauce thickens.

- Turn the heat down and simmer for 15 minutes (and for up to 1 hour if possible).

- Add the cream and bring back to a simmer, and season, immediately before serving.

Variations

- Mushroom sauce: add 2 oz/50 g chopped mushrooms at the simmering stage. Add a teaspoon of chopped parsley at the same stage, if liked.

- Tomato sauce: add 3 tablespoons of tomato purée and 1 tablespoon of chopped basil leaves at the simmering stage.

- Garlic and herb sauce: add 4 cloves of crushed garlic and a selection of chopped fresh herbs 10 minutes before serving.

Plain Wine Sauce

Makes ½ pint/300 ml sauce
1 oz/25 g cornflour
2 tablespoons cold water or red wine
¾ pint/450 ml vegetable stock
salt to taste
white pepper to taste

- Boil the stock in a heavy-bottomed saucepan.

- Mix the cornflour to a thin paste with *cold* water or red wine.

- Use a whisk to ensure that the cornflour paste mixes well with the vegetable stock. The stock should thicken almost immediately.

- Whisk in any extra ingredients – see variations below.

- Turn the heat down and simmer for 12 minutes. Season and serve.

Variations

- Mushroom sauce: add 2 oz/50 g chopped mushrooms.

- Tomato sauce: add 3 tablespoons of tomato purée and 1 tablespoon of chopped basil leaves.

- Garlic and herb sauce: add 4 cloves of crushed garlic and a selection of chopped fresh herbs.

- Orange sauce: add the zest of 1 orange and the juice of 1 lemon.

Rich Wine Sauce

Makes ½ pint/300 ml sauce
1 medium onion, finely chopped
4 oz/100 g mushrooms
½ oz/15 g butter
½ pint/300 ml wine
¼ pint plain wine sauce (see page 153)
2 tablespoons tomato purée

- Fry the onions and the mushrooms in the butter in a heavy-bottomed saucepan. Cook until soft.

- Add the wine and simmer until the volume has been reduced by half.

- Stir in the ready-prepared brown sauce and the tomato purée.

- Bring the sauce back to the boil and then remove from the heat.

- Whisk in any extra ingredients – see variations below.

Variations

- Add 1 tablespoon chopped parsley.

- Add 1 tablespoon chopped tarragon or chopped basil.

- Add 2 cloves of crushed garlic.

Starch Sweets

Cornmeal Pudding

Serves 4
5 oz/150 g yellow cornmeal
¾ pint/450 ml boiling water
1 oz/25 g butter
2 tablespoons black treacle or molasses
1 tablespoon honey
¼ teaspoon ginger
½ teaspoon ground cinnamon
1 egg, beaten
¼ pint/150 ml cream
4 oz/100 g sultanas or raisins
salt to taste

- Place the cornmeal in a saucepan and stir in the boiling water, a little at a time, until all the water has been added.

- Continue to stir over a gentle heat until the mixture thickens and comes to the boil.

- Remove from the heat and stir in the butter, black treacle/molasses, honey and spices.

- Mix the egg with the cream and sultanas/raisins, then quickly stir these into the cooled mixture with the salt, if required.

- Place the mixture in an ovenproof dish.

- Bake at gas mark 4, 350°F, 180°C, for 45 minutes.

- Serve warm.

Baked Bananas

These are ideal for barbecues.

Per person
1 banana, peeled
1 teaspoon honey
1 teaspoon rum
flaked almonds

- Lay each banana on a piece of aluminium foil.

- Dot with honey, and sprinkle rum and flaked almonds.

- Wrap the foil around the banana and lay in an ovenproof dish.

- Bake for 15 minutes in a moderate oven (gas mark 4, 350°F, 180°C)

- Serve with cream.

Variations

- Use preserved stem ginger in place of the honey.

- Baked apples can be cooked in the same way as a protein sweet.

- If you are cooking the bananas on the barbecue place them, in their foil, directly on the barbecue grill.

Dried Fruit Salad

Serves 4
dried dates, apricots, figs, prunes, sultanas (about 8 oz in total)

- Wash the dried fruit to remove any grit.

- Place in a large ovenproof glass bowl and cover with cold water.

- Leave to absorb the water for 12 hours.

- Place in a preheated oven at gas mark 2, 300°F, 150°C and bring slowly to a simmer for 1 hour.

- Serve hot or cold.

Rice Pudding

Serves 4
2 oz/50 g short-grain rice
½ pint/300 ml water
1 oz/25 g molasses or honey
½ pint/300 ml cream
the smallest pinch of saffron
1 tablespoon almonds, chopped
1 tablespoon pistachios, chopped
¼ teaspoon grated nutmeg

- Soak the rice in the water for 1 hour in a saucepan (do not drain).

- Simmer gently for 20 minutes, stirring frequently.

- Transfer to an ovenproof dish, add the molasses/honey, cream and saffron and stir well. Sprinkle the almonds, pistachios and nutmeg on top.

- Bake in the oven at gas mark 2, 300°F, 150°C, for 2 hours.

Brown Bread Pudding

Serves 4
black treacle or molasses – just enough to spread on the bread
8 slices wholemeal bread
butter for greasing
4 oz/100 g dates, well chopped
1 oz/25 g cocoa powder mixed in ½ pint/300 ml water

- Spread a thin layer of treacle on each slice of bread.

- Put 2 slices of bread in the bottom of a greased pie dish.

- Add a layer of dates, then sprinkle with cocoa.

- Add the remaining layers of bread, dates and cocoa.

- Bake in a preheated oven, gas mark 3, 325°F, 160°C, for 20 minutes.

Suet Pudding

Serves 4
8 oz/225 g wholemeal flour
4 oz/100 g dates, chopped
4 oz/100 g suet, chopped
salt to taste
1 egg (optional)
water

- Mix all the dry ingredients together.

- Beat in the egg, if using.

- Add sufficient water for the ingredients to form a soft dough.

- Place the mixture in a 1¾ pint/1 litre pudding bowl.

- Cover the bowl with a sheet of greaseproof paper and then with a clean cotton cloth. Tie securely round, under the lip of the bowl, with string.

- Lower the bowl into a steamer over boiling water and steam for 2 hours.

- Serve hot.

Variations

- Include sultanas, chopped apricots, chopped figs, stem ginger.

- Place 2 tablespoons of molasses in the pudding bowl before adding the soft dough.

❧ CHAPTER 10 ❧
Protein Recipes

● Milk, Cheese, Yogurt, Cream and Eggs ●

One pint of **milk** contains 18 g of high-quality protein, no starch, 28 g of carbohydrate as the sugar lactose and 23 g of fat (28 g=1 oz). It should be used as part of a protein meal.

It is particularly useful as a source of calcium and riboflavin. Most children can drink and digest milk and it contains a useful amount of most vitamins, except for vitamins C and D. It also contains most minerals except iron. Skimmed milk has less than 1.8 per cent fat and has lost most of the fat-soluble vitamins but it retains the same calcium levels as full milk. Heat-treated milk contains fewer vitamins than fresh milk.

Milk should be drunk as fresh as possible, but can stored for up to two days in a refrigerator to preserve the vitamins and prevent microbes from multiplying.

Cow's milk is not suitable for children under one year old unless it has been specially modified. Whole milk, not skimmed or semi-skimmed, can be given to children aged one to two years.

Many adults are unable to digest the lactose in milk except in small quantities, and yogurt or cheese can provide the same calcium and vitamins.

Cheese is formed from the milk protein, casein, and still contains most of the protein, fat and vitamin A of milk. It has lost most of the lactose and the B vitamins. Fromage frais is a low-fat soft cheese that retains high levels of calcium.

Yogurt is nutritionally similar to milk, except that the lactose level has been reduced. It still contains excellent levels of protein, calcium and riboflavin. Fat levels can vary from 0.2–9 per cent according to the type of milk used. Yogurts often have added flavourings and sugar, but plain yogurts, to which you add your own flavourings, give you the greatest control over the nutritional content.

Single cream and **whipping cream** are 19.1 per cent fat and **double cream** is 48 per cent fat. It still contains vitamins A, E and D.

Eggs contain 12.5 per cent protein and 10.8 per cent fat and contribute useful amounts of vitamins D, retinol, riboflavin and the minerals iodine and iron. The iron is best absorbed when eaten with a meal that contains plenty of vitamin C.

	protein	starch	sugar	fat	calcium/100 g
Whole milk	3.2%		4.8%	2.4%	115mg
Yogurt, full-fat	5.7%		7.8%	3%	200mg
Skimmed milk	3.3%		5%	0.1%	120mg
Cream, single	2.6%		4.1%	19.1%	91mg
Cheddar	25.5%			34.4%	720mg
Brie	19.3%			26.9%	540mg
Eggs	12.5%			10.8%	57mg

• Pulses: Dried Beans and Peas •

Pulses are an excellent source of protein, calcium, potassium, iron, the B vitamins and niacin. Dried beans should never be eaten raw, because of the poisons that they contain. Kidney beans, for example, contain a toxin called haemagglutinin, which is only destroyed by soaking for at least eight hours, followed by fast boiling for 10–15 minutes; and soya beans contain a trypsin inhibitor, which needs soaking for 12 hours, a rapid boil for one hour for its destruction, and simmering for a further two hours. The soaking water should be discarded. A pressure cooker is very useful to reduce the cooking times for these pulses.

Only mung beans, split peas and lentils can be cooked

without soaking first, but they still need boiling for 40 minutes.

Microwave and slow cookers are not suitable for pulses, unless they have been soaked and vigorously boiled for 10 minutes first.

Pulses should always be cooked in unsalted water – salt makes them tough. They do not keep indefinitely, and are far better fresh.

Sprouting beans produce vitamin C and alter and improve the balance of nutrients, so they can be considered as a vegetable. Good sprouting beans are aduki, whole lentils, mung beans and chickpeas.

Gram flour is produced by grinding a variety of beans. Mung bean and lentil flours are the most easily digested.

Pulses often cause digestive problems. The amount that a person can eat at one meal and digest in comfort is very limited – 1 oz/25 g of dried pulses per day will be the limit for most people. Some people find soya beans particularly indigestible and bitter. Dried pulses fit in best as a meal with vegetables only, or as part of a protein meal.

• Soya Protein Products: Tofu •

Because soya beans are a good source of protein, but need such careful and prolonged preparation, products made from tofu have evolved which make them easier to use.

Tofu is soya bean curd. The beans are soaked and then ground to a paste. The soluble sugars and proteins are then washed out and gypsum is added to the liquid to precipitate out the protein as a white solid. It can be kept refrigerated in an airtight container full of water for up to four days.

Tofu has little taste but absorbs the flavours of herbs and spices to produce excellent protein meals.

	protein	starch	sugar	fat/oil	calcium/100 g
Tofu	8.1%	0.2%	0.3%	4.2%	510 mg

Texturized vegetable protein is manufactured by extracting protein from a range of plants, including soya, artificially fortifying it with a range of vitamins and minerals, and then reforming it into chunks. It is probably more healthy to eat the wide range of vegetables!

• Protein Miscellaneous •

Dhal

Dhal can be made using a variety of mung beans, split peas and lentils. Wash the pulses well before use and check for any small stones or grit.

Serves 4
1 oz/225 g lentils
1 bay leaf
2 cloves garlic, crushed
1 teaspoon fresh ginger, finely chopped
1 small onion, finely chopped
1 pint/600 ml water
½ teaspoon cumin seeds
2 tablespoons olive oil
salt to taste

- Put the lentils, bay leaf, garlic, ginger and onion in the water in a heavy-bottomed saucepan.

- Bring to the boil and simmer on minimum heat for 45 minutes.

- Just before serving, fry the cumin seeds briefly in the olive oil and then stir the cumin seeds and oil and the salt into the dhal.

- Serve hot with a selection of vegetables or crudités.

Variations

- Use a selection of other flavourings, such as ground asafoe-tida, turmeric, coriander, fenugreek, mustard seed, garam masala, cayenne pepper, lemon, lime, tamarind paste. Try with ¼ teaspoonful of each of your selection to start with.

Hummus

Serves 4
8 oz/225 g chickpeas
5 cloves garlic
1 small onion, finely chopped
2 tablespoons olive oil
6 oz/175 g sesame seeds
3 lemons
salt to taste

- Wash the chickpeas and then soak overnight in 2 pints/1 l water, drain and then wash again.

- Boil the chickpeas vigorously for 10 minutes in at least a pint of fresh water and then simmer for 2 hours until tender (or boil in a pressure cooker at high pressure for 30 minutes).

- Drain the peas and discard the water.

- Blend the garlic, onion, olive oil and sesame seeds with half the lemon juice to a purée in a blender.

- Add the cooked chickpeas a few at a time to the purée in the blender, adding the remaining lemon juice as required. Reduce to a smooth purée after each addition.

- Serve the hummus hot or cold with a range of vegetables or crudités.

• Bean Salad •

All beans must be properly cooked before being used to make salads. Beans with thick skins should have their skins removed. All beans can be used for salads in this way. Try mixtures of different beans.

The cooked beans should be tossed in a dressing and then left to marinade for an hour before being served cold.

The simplest dressing is one made of olive oil and lemon or lime juice, but any starch-free dressing can be used to create a wide variety of bean salads.

Red Bean Salad

Serves 4
8 oz/225 g red kidney beans
3 oz/75 g shelled walnuts
1 oz/25 g garlic cloves, peeled and crushed
1 tablespoon lemon juice
2 tablespoons olive oil
2 tablespoons fresh coriander leaves, finely chopped
salt and pepper to taste

- Soak the beans for at least 8 hours in cold water, then rinse.

- Add fresh water and fast-boil the beans for 10–15 minutes.

- Simmer the beans for a further 2 hours and drain.

- Reduce the walnuts to a flour with a pestle and mortar or use a coffee grinder.

- Liquidize the garlic in the lemon juice.

- Combine the walnut flour with the garlic in the mortar and blend in the olive oil to form a smooth paste. Add a little more oil if needed.

- Toss the beans in the dressing and leave to stand for 1 hour.

- Season and sprinkle the fresh coriander leaves over the top just before serving.

Bean and Chickpea Salad – pressure cooker

Pressure cooking is especially useful for pulses and dried beans, as it reduces the cooking time so much. It also thoroughly destroys the toxins found in some dried beans.

Serves 4
4 oz/100 g chickpeas
4 oz/100 g haricot beans
4 oz/100 g dried red kidney beans
olive oil and herb dressing
2 tablespoons olive oil
½ tablespoon fresh basil, chopped
½ tablespoon fresh marjoram, chopped
½ tablespoon fresh coriander, chopped
½ tablespoon fresh thyme, chopped
½ tablespoon fresh parsley, chopped
1 onion, chopped

- Soak the chick peas and haricot beans overnight, keeping the kidney beans separate. (The soaking time can be shortened to 1 hour by using boiling water.) Drain.

- Put the kidney beans in the unperforated basket of a pressure cooker and cover with fresh water. Put the haricot beans and chickpeas together in the remaining part of the cooker and cover with water. Season both sections. The trivet is not needed. Cook under high pressure (15 lb/16.75 kg) for 20 minutes. Cool slowly.

- Make the dressing by blending all the remaining ingredients except the onion together using a pestle and mortar or a blender.

- Drain the beans when cool enough to handle and mix together in a bowl. Add the chopped onion. Toss the beans in the dressing and leave to cool.

- Serve cold.

Almond Crackers – *no* starch

These are an excellent way of serving cheese without the starch!

Makes 15 small crackers
4 oz/100 g sesame seeds
1 oz/25 g sunflower seeds
4 oz/100 g ground almonds
¼ pint/150 ml warm water as required

- Grind the sesame and sunflower seeds to a smooth paste.

- Mix in the ground almonds, with a little water, until a uniform paste is formed – add as little water as possible.

- Knead for 10–15 minutes to form a smooth dough.

- Roll out thinly and cut into squares.

- Place the crackers on a greased tray.

- Bake in a preheated oven, gas mark 6, 400°F, 200°C, for 8–12 minutes until golden brown.

- Turn out onto a wire tray to cool and dry.

- Keep crackers in an airtight container.

Cheese Crackers

Makes 15 small crackers
4 oz/100 g ground almonds
4 oz/100 g groundnuts (peanuts)
4 oz/100 g cheese (Cheddar or similar), grated
¼ pint/150 ml warm water

- Mix all the ingredients until a uniform dough is formed – add as little water as possible.

- Knead for 10–15 minutes to form a smooth dough.

- Roll out thinly and cut into squares.

- Place the crackers on a greased tray.

- Bake in a preheated oven, gas mark 6, 400°F, 200°C, for 8–12 minutes until golden brown.

- Cool before turning out onto a wire tray.

- Keep crackers in an airtight container.

Cheese Omelette

Omelettes are best eaten immediately after cooking and served hot. If you are cooking for several people, they will need to be served and eaten as they are cooked, not kept until everyone can be served together.

Serves 1 or 2
2 eggs
1 tablespoon chives, chopped
salt and freshly ground black pepper to taste
1 tablespoon olive oil
2 oz/50 g cheese, thinly sliced

- Beat the eggs and stir in the chives, salt and pepper.
- Heat the grill.
- Heat the olive oil in a frying pan and when hot, pour in the beaten eggs.
- Immediately place the cheese slices on top of the omelette.
- As soon as the omelette is almost cooked underneath place the frying pan under the grill until the cheese melts. (Don't put the handle under the grill!)
- Flip the sides of the omelette to the centre and serve immediately.

Variations

- Add 1 tomato, sliced thinly, before placing the cheese on top.
- Add 2 oz/50 g mushrooms, sliced thinly, before placing the cheese on top.
- Beat the yolks and the whites separately before folding them together. This makes a lighter omelette.
- For a herb omelette, add chopped fresh parsley and chopped fresh marjoram.
- Add several chopped olives.
- For a soufflé omelette, beat the whites separately until stiff, then fold into the beaten yolks. Finish under the grill to toast the top.

Cheese Pudding

Serves 4
4 eggs
8 oz/225 g Cheddar cheese, grated
2 oz/50 g gram flour
½ pint/300 ml milk
1 oz/25 g fresh ground mustard seed
Salt and freshly ground black pepper to taste
2 tomatoes, thinly sliced

- Beat the eggs and then beat in the remaining ingredients, except the tomatoes.

- Place the mixture in a greased baking dish.

- Place the sliced tomato on top and bake for 20 minutes in a preheated oven, gas mark 6, 400°F, 200°C.

• Cheese and Vegetables •

Many vegetables go well with a variety of cheeses. The vegetable should be cooked until just tender, and then cooked briefly with the cheese sauce. Many vegetables can be eaten raw, and these need only be cooked sufficiently with the cheese to heat them through.

Cheeses such as Edam produce a mild, if stringy, sauce, while the Cheddars produce stronger-flavoured sauces and the blue cheeses produce the strongest flavours of all.

Vegetables can also be served with hot or cold cream cheese or fromage frais, and many countries serve thinly sliced cold vegetables in yogurt.

Cheese and Vegetable Bake

Serves 4
4 oz/100 g cheese (Cheddar or a blue cheese), grated or crumbled
2 large carrots, grated
1 small cauliflower, chopped
2 oz/50 g Chinese leaves, finely sliced
2 oz/50 g onion, finely sliced
2 oz/50 g fresh green peas
2 oz/50 g mushrooms, chopped

- Mix all the ingredients together and place in an ovenproof dish.

- Bake for 20 minutes in a preheated oven, gas mark 6, 400°F, 200°C.

Bubble and Squeak

This traditional dish makes excellent use of odds and ends of vegetables and meat, all bound together with an egg and then fried.

Add a few extra vegetables to ensure there is plenty of variety.

Per person
cold cooked meat
cold cooked vegetables
1 egg
grated cheese

- Chop the cold meat and vegetables, then mix together.

- Beat the egg and stir into the cold meat and vegetables.

- Fry over a moderate heat for 10–15 minutes, turning after 5 minutes.

- Sprinkle with grated cheese and brown the top under the grill before serving.

Mish-Mash

Another good meal for using up leftovers. Any of the ingredients can be varied, so long as no starch is used.

onion, chopped
butter or olive oil
chicken pieces
4 oz/100g mushrooms, uncooked
green vegetable (cabbage, broccoli)
cream
chicken stock or gravy
root vegetables (swede, carrot, parsnip)
grated cheese

- Sauté the onion in a little butter or olive oil.

- Put the chicken pieces at the bottom of a casserole dish. Add the mushrooms, onion and green vegetable.

- Mix a dash of cream and stock or gravy together to a thick consistency, then pour over the vegetables so that they are just covered.

- Mash or purée the root vegetables, spread over the top and sprinkle with grated cheese.

- Bake in a moderate oven, gas mark 6, 400°F, 200°C, for 20 minutes until hot through and golden on top.

Protein Soups

Beef Stock

2 lb/900 g beef marrowbones
2 pints/1.2 litres water
1 onion, sliced
1 carrot, sliced
1 bay leaf
4 black peppercorns, whole
salt to taste

- Place the marrowbones and water in a pressure cooker and simmer gently for 15 minutes. Then cool and remove any scum that forms on the surface.

- Add the remaining ingredients and cook under high pressure for 45 minutes before allowing to cool: without a pressure cooker, simmer the bones gently for 4 hours.

- Cool, strain the stock and leave to go cold. Then remove the solid fat from the surface.

- Freeze the stock in small quantities for later use in soups, stews and sauces.

Variations

- Chicken/turkey stock: follow the same recipe using a chicken/turkey carcass or 8 oz/225 g chicken/turkey giblets.

- Fish stock: follow the same recipe using 1 lb/450 g fish trimmings.

Cauliflower and Cheese Soup

Serves 4
1 onion
½ cauliflower
pinch of thyme
salt and freshly ground pepper to taste
½ pint/300 ml chicken stock
4 oz/100 g fromage frais or grated cheese
½ pint/300 ml milk

- Cook the onion, cauliflower, thyme and seasoning until soft in the stock.

- Mash these up with a potato masher or use a food processor.

- Stir in the fromage frais/grated cheese and the milk.

- Heat the soup until hot enough to serve but do not boil. This should be a fairly thick soup.

Scotch Broth

Serves 4
1 medium onion, well chopped
1 medium leek, well washed and cut into rings
2 medium carrots, thinly sliced
1 small turnip or swede, chopped
salt and freshly ground black pepper to taste
1 pint/600 ml mutton stock
parsley, chopped, to garnish

- Add all the ingredients to the stock. Bring to the boil and simmer gently for 1 hour.

- Garnish with the parsley.

Chicken Soup – pressure cooker

Serves 4
1 chicken carcass, cooked
2 pints/1.2 litres water
salt and freshly ground black pepper
1 onion, sliced
2 cloves garlic, chopped or crushed
2 carrots, chopped
1 celery stick, sliced
1 small turnip, swede or parsnip, chopped
4 oz/100 g orange lentils
1 tablespoon chopped tarragon or ½ teaspoon dried tarragon
1 tablespoon chopped parsley

- Remove all meat from the carcass and set aside.

- Put the bones into the pressure cooker and cover with the water. Add the seasoning.

- Replace the lid and bring to high pressure.

- Remove the carcass and take off any additional meat. Set this aside.

- To the liquor now in the cooker, add the remaining ingredients except the parsley and chicken meat, seal the cooker and heat to high pressure.

- Cook for 20 minutes under high pressure.

- Reduce the pressure, add all the chicken meat and the parsley, and bring to the boil before serving.

Bacon Soup – pressure cooker

Serves 4
1 small bacon knuckle
1 onion, sliced
2 cloves garlic, chopped or crushed
2 carrots, chopped
1 turnip
4 oz/100 g orange lentils
1 tablespoon chopped tarragon or ½ teaspoon dried tarragon
1 tablespoon chopped parsley
do not add salt

- Soak the bacon knuckle overnight in cold water. Drain and wash in cold water.

- Boil covered but unsealed in fresh water for 5 minutes. Remove from the water and take off the thick skin with a sharp knife.

- Replace the knuckle in the pressure cooker and cover with 2 pints/1.2 litres water.

- Add the remaining ingredients, replace the lid and bring to high pressure.

- Cook according to the weight of the knuckle at 12 minutes per lb/450 g.

- This is more like a stew than a soup and should be served as a main meal.

• Protein Snacks and Starters •

Avocado Pear with Soft Cheese

This is a nice starter for a protein meal.

Serves 4
2 avocado pears
4 oz/100 g soft cream cheese
1 tablespoon double cream
1 tablespoon white wine
½ teaspoon freshly ground coriander seeds
½ teaspoon freshly ground cardamon seeds
salt and pepper

- Halve the avocados and remove the stones.

- Blend the remaining ingredients and fill the cavities.

- Serve with a salad garnish.

- Tip: keep a separate peppermill for coriander seeds and grind as necessary.

Warm Crispy Chicken Salad

Serves 4
skin of 1 chicken, cut into pieces the size of potato crisps
1 head of lettuce, shredded
½ cucumber, cut into cubes
4 tomatoes, cut into quarters
8 radishes, sliced
4 tablespoons spicy mayonnaise (see page 219)
1 oz/25 g pine kernels, toasted

- Fry the chicken skin gently until all the fat is taken out and the skin is crisp.

- Meanwhile, prepare the salad and arrange in a bowl or individual bowls, leaving a depression in the centre.

- Pile the chicken skins in the centre while still hot, pour spicy mayonnaise over and top with pine kernels. Serve at once.

Crab and Avocado Mousse

An excellent starter for a protein meal.

Serves 4
2 avocado pears
6 oz/175 g can crabmeat
¼ pint/150 ml fish or chicken stock
1 oz/25 g butter
5 oz/150 ml double cream
3 tablespoons white wine
½ oz/15 g gelatine
½ pint/300 ml mayonnaise
garnish of prawns, cucumber, lemon (sliced) or fresh parsley

- Halve the avocados and scoop the flesh out of the skins. Mash with a fork or in a blender.

- Drain the crabmeat and add the liquid to the stock.

- Flake the crabmeat and add to the mashed avocado.

- Melt the butter in a pan, stir in 1 tablespoon of cream and simmer gently for 1 minute. Stir in the stock and simmer for a further 2 minutes.

- Remove from the heat and fold the crab and avocado mixture into the sauce.

- Warm the wine and dissolve the gelatine in it, then stir in the avocado mixture.

- Whip the remaining cream lightly and fold into the avocado mixture with the mayonnaise.

- Spoon the mixture into a mould or ramekins and chill until set.

- Turn out and serve, garnished with prawns, cucumber slices, lemon slices or fresh parsley.

Quiche Lorraine

Flans and quiches are easily prepared without pastry. Originally the pastry was not intended to be eaten, but was used merely as a clean and waterproof container for the ingredients while they cooked.

Serves 4
3 oz/75 g Cheddar cheese, grated
6 bacon rashers, sliced
2 onions, chopped
1 tablespoon olive oil
2 large eggs
¼ pint/150 ml milk
salt and pepper to taste
3 tomatoes, sliced

- Use an ovenware flan dish. Sprinkle half the cheese on the bottom of the flan dish.

- Fry the bacon and onion together in the oil until just cooked and spread over the cheese.

- Beat together the eggs, milk and seasoning, pour over the mixture and then sprinkle the rest of the cheese on top. Lay the sliced tomatoes on top.

- Bake at gas mark 5, 375°F, 190°C for 30 minutes until set.

Variations

- For a richer mixture, mix cream with the milk, or use evaporated milk in place of the milk or milk and cream.

- For a wide range of different fillings replace the cheese, onion and bacon:

- Mushroom quiche: use 6 oz/175 g mushrooms, sliced – no need to fry first.

- Herb quiche: use 2 tablespoons mixed fresh herbs, chopped – marjoram, basil, thyme, for example.

- Prawn and onion quiche: use 6 spring onions, trimmed and chopped, and 6 oz/175 g peeled prawns.

- Ham and sweetcorn quiche: use 6 slices of ham, fried, and 8 oz/225 g sweetcorn, cooked.

- Salmon quiche: use one 8 oz/225 g can salmon or flaked, fresh cooked salmon.

- Tuna and cheese quiche: use one 8 oz/225 g can tuna and 2 oz/150 g cheese – sprinkle over the top after adding the egg mixture.

- Spanish quiche: add cooked peas, sweetcorn, sliced red and green peppers, tomatoes.

• Protein Main Meals •

Fish and Shellfish

Fish and shellfish are an excellent source of first-class protein, and some fish are a valuable source of fats and fat-soluble vitamins, such as A and D. They also provide an important source of minerals, particularly iodine, and the bones of canned sardines and salmon provide calcium and phosphorus.

Fresh fish should appear bright and clear, with the gills still red. Frozen fish is often better-quality than fresh, from an open counter, but processed fish often includes variable amounts of water.

Frozen fish should be thawed in a refrigerator rather than at room temperature. Fresh fish should be gutted and cleaned as soon as possible, washed well in cold water and then drained. Skin with large, prominent scales should be removed.

The domestic refrigerator is too warm to keep fish fresh. Ideally it should be packed in crushed ice for no more than a day or frozen immediately.

The best methods of cooking fish are poaching and steaming, which ensure that the maximum nutritional value is retained, provided the juice from the cooked fish is also eaten. Baking, frying or grilling fish can destroy up to 30 per cent of the B vitamins. Fish should not be cooked in batter. Moist cooking methods are often the best.

Sole, plaice, dab and **flounder** are the smaller flat-fish, often cooked whole, and best between May and February. They contain almost no fat and are easily overcooked.

Brill, halibut and turbot are larger and generally cut into steaks, but require a moist cooking method.

Cod, coley, haddock, hake, pollack and whiting are white-fleshed fish. Their quality is best between June and February. They are best steamed or poached.

Salmon and **trout** contain up to 10 per cent fat, depending on the season. They can be fried or grilled, but dry out quickly if overcooked.

Herring, mackerel and **sardine** are the oiliest fish and excellent sources of vitamins D and E. They are best fried or grilled.

Tuna and **swordfish** contain up to 5 per cent oils, if fresh, but canned tuna contains little oil.

Cartilaginous fish are all good sources of vitamin E and excellent for young children, as these fish contain no bones. **Ray** and **skate** are best cooked moist. **Dogfish** and **shark** need to be skinned before cooking. The flesh is firmer than most fish and they can be grilled or stewed.

Crustaceans are a particularly good source of minerals, especially iron. **Lobster** and **crab** must be eaten very fresh. They should be purchased still alive and killed by dropping into boiling water. The head sac and intestine need to be removed before cooking, and the gills discarded after cooking. **Prawns** and **shrimps** should also be eaten as fresh as possible.

Molluscs such as **oysters** and **mussels** are also excellent sources of minerals. They should be alive when cooked. The safest source is tinned mussels.

Baked Fish

Most types of fish can be baked and should retain their shape.

Method 1

- Brush the fish with olive oil and place in an ovenproof dish.

- Add 1 tablespoon of white wine or fish stock for each portion of fish.

- Brush a little more olive oil or butter over the upper surface of the fish.

- Cover the dish with foil.

- Bake in a preheated oven, gas mark 4, 350°F, 180°C, until cooked, which depends on thickness: thin fillets, 8–2 minutes; small whole fish or thicker fillets, 15–20 minutes; whole large fish, 25–30 minutes.

- The fish is cooked when the thickest flesh is translucent all the way through.

Method 2

- Take and oil a piece of foil large enough to enclose the fish.

- Place the fish in the middle of the foil and cover with dabs of butter, herbs and seasoning.

- Fold the foil over to seal it above the fish.

- Bake in a preheated oven, gas mark 5, 375°F, 190°C until cooked, which depends on thickness: thin fillets, 8–12 minutes; small whole fish or thicker fillets, 15–20 minutes; whole large fish, 25–30 minutes.

Mackerel Baked in Foil

Per person
1 medium-sized mackerel
1 teaspoon wholegrain mustard
1 tablespoon gooseberries
1 tablespoon flaked almonds
1 teaspoon chopped fresh fennel

- Clean and wash the mackerel.

- Fillet by opening up the fish, laying it open side down on a slab, and running your thumb down the backbone. This will remove most of the bones.

- Spread the cavity of the mackerel with wholegrain mustard.

- Place as many gooseberries as will fit inside the cavity.

- Take a piece of foil large enough to enclose the fish.

- Place the fish in the middle, sprinkle with the flaked almonds and fennel and then fold the foil over to seal it above the fish.

- Bake in a preheated oven, gas mark 5, 375°F, 190°C, for 15–20 minutes until cooked, which depends on thickness.

- The fish is cooked when the thickest flesh is translucent.

Variation

- Add several whole, peeled cloves of garlic inside each fish. These will bake to a soft mash and can be spread over the fish during eating.

- This recipe works well in a pressure cooker: cook under high pressure for 4 minutes.

Grilled Fish

Round fish grill well, but white fish fillets dry out easily.

Crisp the skin first by grilling briefly under a fierce heat, then reduce the heat to medium and grill more slowly until cooked.

Cooking time depends on the thickness of the fish. Allow 6 minutes each side for a small fish and up to 10 minutes each side for a larger fish.

It is easy to overcook grilled fish, so watch it carefully and remove from the grill as soon as the thickest flesh comes away from the bone.

Grilled Shark

Per person
1 shark steak
olive oil, butter or garlic butter
2 cloves garlic

- Wash the shark steak in cold water. It can also be skinned at this stage.

- Brush the steak with a little olive oil, butter or garlic butter.

- Grill under a medium heat until cooked – up to 10 minutes each side, depending on the thickness of the steak.

- Brush with crushed garlic immediately before serving.

Poached Fish

Poaching is the best cooking method for most types of fish. Placed the cleaned fish in a pan or ovenproof dish that fits the fish closely. Cover with cold water, milk, fish stock or white wine. Bring the pan to a gentle boil, either in the oven or on the hob. Then reduce the heat to keep the temperature just at a simmer, not boiling.

Cooking time depends on thickness and is taken from the

start of boiling: thin fillets, 8–12 minutes; small whole fish or thicker fillets, 15–20 minutes; whole large fish, 25–30 minutes.

Drain the fish before serving and use the liquid in the preparation of a sauce.

Poached Skate Wings

Per person
1 small skate wing or ½ large wing
enough milk to cover the wing
fresh herbs (fennel, rosemary, bay, basil)
salt and pepper to taste

- Place the skate wings in one layer in a pan, with as little overlap as possible. The pan should have a close-fitting lid.

- Add the milk.

- Sprinkle with herbs and salt and pepper.

- Bring the milk to a simmer and cover with the lid.

- Turn the fish after 5 minutes.

- Continue to simmer gently for 10–15 minutes until cooked – the flesh lifts easily from the cartilage but the cartilage does not fall apart.

- Use the milk to make a sauce or fish soup (freeze until required).

Salmon Pie

Other fish can be used, but salmon is the most delicious!

Serves 4
1 lb/450 g salmon, cooked or tinned
8 oz/225 g mushrooms, sliced
6 oz/175 g peas, cooked
6 oz/175 g sweetcorn, cooked
1 leek
1 oz/25 g butter
7 fl oz/200 ml milk
1 glass white wine
2 tablespoons fresh mayonnaise
3 oz/75 g cheese, grated

- Flake the salmon into a casserole dish and cover with the mushrooms, peas and sweetcorn.

- Slice the leek and fry gently in the butter for five minutes.

- Add the milk slowly and allow to simmer until the leek is cooked.

- Remove from the heat and add the wine and mayonnaise.

- Stir in 2 oz/50 g cheese and pour over the salmon and vegetables.

- Sprinkle with the remaining cheese and bake in a moderate oven, gas mark 5, 375°F, 190°C, for 20–30 minutes until hot through and golden on top.

• Meat •

Meat protein provides the full range of essential amino acids and is the largest dietary source of vitamins, iron and zinc. Visible fat should be removed, unless other sources of fat in the diet are kept to a minimum.

Uncooked meat should be eaten fresh, but it can kept in the bottom of a domestic refrigerator, below any cooked meat, for a couple of days.

Beef, mutton, lamb and **pork** have the highest fat content. The highest-priced cuts of meat are often the tenderest and require the least cooking, but slow, moist cooking methods will produce excellent meals from all cuts. The nutritional value is the same for all cuts of meat, but pork, bacon and ham are particularly rich in thiamin.

Chicken, goose and **duck** store most of their fat in a layer under the skin and in the body cavity. This fat and the skin can be removed before cooking, or the cooking method must ensure that all the fat melts and is able to drain away. If the fat is removed first, moist cooking methods should be used or the meat will be dry and tough. **Turkey** rarely contains much fat, and fat may need to be added for roasting. Pressure cooking is one of the best methods for low-fat meat.

Rabbit, hare and **venison** contain little fat and, without due care, the meat will end up dry and tough. Use slow, moist cooking methods, or add a small amount of fat when cooking.

Liver and **kidney** are the best sources of iron in the diet, with high levels of many vitamins. They should be cooked as little as possible. Women should not eat liver during the early stages of pregnancy.

Sweetbreads and **tripe** are easily digested and useful sources of protein.

Sausages

Commercial sausages are often mixtures of one-third starch, one-third meat and one-third fat.

Home-made sausages are easy to make using good quality meat and herbs. We use the International King Chef Sausage Maker from Wrightway Marketing Ltd, Peterborough, PE1 5TX. Skins are available from good kitchen shops or by mail order from the same firm.

Fresh meat binds together very easily, and cereals and

binders are not necessary to produce a good sausage, although an egg can be added to the mixture if desired. Natural skins produce a strong, gently curved sausage but need to be soaked to soften them, before they are filled. Man-made skins or casings do not require any washing or soaking and are the easiest to use.

Sausages that remain moist on cooking need a fairly high fat content. Pig's-back fat, fresh beef suet or minced belly pork can be used. These sausages should be used fresh as they contain no preservatives.

Sausages made with fresh ingredients can be frozen until required for use.

Pork Sausages

Makes 1 b/450 g sausages
1 lb/450 g minced belly pork
2 teaspoons fresh mixed herbs (sage, rosemary and thyme) or 1 teaspoon mixed dried herbs
salt and freshly ground black pepper to taste
½ teaspoon allspice

- Blend the ingredients together by beating the pork into the herbs, seasoning and spices with a food processor, or use the back of a spoon until the mixture sticks in a ball.

- Place this mixture in the barrel of the sausage-maker.

- Fit a 1½ inch/4 cm length of compacted wide casing over the nozzle of the sausage-maker and tie a knot in the open end.

- Extrude the mixture as a paste into the skins, refilling the sausage-maker as required. Do not overfill the skins or they will burst on cooking.

- Tie knots in the open end of the skins and then twist the sausage at intervals to produce individual sausages. It is best not to cut these apart until after they have been cooked.

- Sausages should be cooked slowly and not be pricked.

- They can be baked for 30–40 minutes in a preheated oven, gas mark 4, 350°F, 180°C.

- They can be grilled under a medium heat for 20–25 minutes. Turn them at intervals to allow even cooking.

- They can also be fried over a low heat for 20–25 minutes. Turn them at intervals to allow even cooking.

Beef and Tomato Sausages

Makes 1 lb/450 g sausages
12 oz/350 g minced beef
4 oz/100 g minced belly pork
1 tablespoon tomato purée
2 teaspoons fresh herbs or 1 teaspoon dried herbs
salt and freshly ground black pepper to taste

- Follow the instructions for Pork Sausages (see page 188)

Turkey and Garlic Sausages

Makes 1 lb/450 g sausages
12 oz/350 g minced turkey
4 oz/100 g minced belly pork
2 cloves fresh garlic, grated
2 teaspoons fresh herbs or 1 teaspoon dried herbs
salt and freshly ground black pepper to taste

- Follow instructions for Pork Sausages (see page 188)

Chipolata Sausages

Makes 1 lb/450 g sausages
12 oz/350 g minced pork
4 oz/100 g minced belly pork
1 oz/25 g gram flour
1 tablespoon water
1 small pinch each of fresh coriander and thyme leaves
1 small pinch each of pimento and grated nutmeg
salt and freshly ground black pepper to taste

- Use the smaller chipolata skins for these sausages.

- Follow the instructions for Pork Sausages (see page 188)

Pork and Apple Sausages

Makes 1 lb/450 g sausages
10 oz/275 g minced pork
4 oz/100 g minced belly pork
4 oz/100 g cooking apple
2 teaspoons fresh herbs or 1 teaspoon dried herbs
salt and freshly ground black pepper to taste

- Follow the instructions for Pork Sausages (see page 188)

Pies and Stews

Turkey Moussaka

Serves 4
1 aubergine, sliced
salt
olive oil for frying
4 oz/100 g mushrooms, sliced
1 onion, chopped
2 garlic cloves, peeled and crushed
herbs (basil, thyme, sage)
1 lb/450 g turkey mince
sea salt and freshly ground black pepper to taste
¼ pint/150 ml turkey stock, vegetable stock or water
For the cheese sauce:
1 egg
¼ pint/150 ml milk
4 oz/100 g Cheddar cheese, grated
1 teaspoon dry mustard or wholegrain mustard

- Place the aubergine slices in a colander, sprinkle with salt and leave for 30 minutes. Rinse in cold water and drain.

- Heat some olive oil gently in a large frying pan. Fry the aubergine slices until golden on each side. Remove and set aside. Fry the mushrooms until soft. Set aside.

- Fry the onion until translucent.

- Add the garlic, herbs and turkey mince and fry until the meat is sealed on all sides.

- Add the sea salt and pepper to taste.

- Layer the meat mixture with the mushrooms and aubergines in a casserole dish, finishing off with mushrooms and aubergines.

- Pour the stock over the mixture in the casserole.

- For the cheese sauce, beat the egg and milk together.

- Simmer gently over a low heat until the mixture begins to thicken.

- Add 3 oz/75 g of the grated cheese, the mustard and more salt and pepper to taste.

- Simmer gently for a few more minutes, then pour over the moussaka.

- Sprinkle with the remaining cheese.

- Cook for 30 minutes at gas mark 6, 400°F, 200°C until the top is golden.

Variations

- Add tomato paste or puréed tomatoes to the meat mixture.

- For a traditional moussaka, used minced lamb instead of turkey, but remember that it is more fatty.

Cottage Pie

Serves 4
4 medium carrots
1 small swede
2 medium onions
olive for frying
1 lb/450 g mince
¼ pint/150 ml beef stock or 14 oz/400 g tin tomatoes
2 cloves garlic, crushed
salt and freshly ground black pepper to taste
sliced tomato for garnish

- Cook and mash the carrots and swede together.

- Chop the onion and fry in a little olive oil until it is translucent.

- Add the mince to the frying pan and cook for 8 minutes over a moderate heat. Stir while cooking.

- Add the stock or tinned tomatoes and crushed garlic to the mince and bring to a simmer. Season to taste.

- Transfer the mince and tomato to a casserole.

- Place the mashed swede and carrot as a layer over the mince.

- Add sliced tomato to decorate the top before baking.

- Bake for 20 minutes in a preheated oven, gas mark 6, 400°F, 200°C.

Beef Stew

Serves 4
1 lb/450 g shin of beef
1 tablespoon olive oil
1 large onion
1 oz/25 g mushrooms
2 large carrots
½ pint/300 ml beef stock
1 bay leaf
salt and freshly ground black pepper to taste

- Slice the meat into ½ inch/1 cm cubes and then brown in a hot frying pan with a little of the olive oil.

- Chop the onion, mushrooms and carrots, and then fry them briefly in the oil.

- Place the beef and vegetables with the stock in an ovenproof dish.

- Add the herb and seasoning.

- Bring to a simmer over a low heat.

- Cover with a tight lid and cook slowly in the oven, at gas mark 1, 275°F, 140°C, for 3 hours.

- Check at intervals to make sure the stew is simmering gently and add water if required.

• Roasting Meat •

Cooking times for tender joints

- Beef on the bone – 15 minutes per lb/450g and 15 minutes extra.

- Beef without a bone, and for lamb and mutton – 20 minutes per lb/450g and 20 minutes extra.

- Pork and veal – 25 minutes per lb/450g and 25 minutes extra.

Instructions

- Place the meat in a roasting tin on the middle shelf of a hot oven, at gas mark 7, 425°F, 220°C.

- After 20 minutes turn the heat down to moderately hot, gas mark 5, 375°F, 190°C.

- Baste the joint with hot dripping at intervals or place an extra strip of fat over the joint while it is cooking, unless the meat has its own layer of fat on top.

- Stand the joint in a warm place for 10–15 minutes before serving.

Less tender meat

- This should be roasted at a lower temperature, gas mark 4, 350°F, 180°C.

- Allow a total cooking time of 35 minutes per 1b/450g and 35 minutes extra.

Pot roasting

- Ideal for less tender meat. Placed the meat in a saucepan with a tight-fitting lid. Put sufficient dripping or lard with the meat and fry it, turning until it is browned all over.

- Put the lid in place and reduce the heat to simmer until the meat is cooked.

- Allow a total cooking time of 45 minutes per 1b/450g.

Pressure cooking meat is another quick and easy method.

Roast Chicken

- Frozen chicken must be completely thawed before cooking starts.

- Remove any neck or giblets.

- Wash the prepared chicken in cold water, both inside and out, and allow to drain.

- Place the meat in a roasting tin on the middle shelf of a hot oven, gas mark 7, 425°F, 220°C.

- After 20 minutes turn the heat down to moderately hot, gas mark 5, 375°F, 190°C.

- For chicken and duck allow a total cooking time of 15 minutes per lb/450g and 15 minutes extra.

- To test if the bird is cooked, pull at the junction between the thigh joint and the body. If the juices here run clear and the meat at the joint starts to separate from the bone, then the bird is cooked. If the juices are still pink, then cook for longer.

- The juices that run out of the body cavity should also be clear, not pink.

Roast Turkey

- A family of four needs an oven-ready turkey weighing 8–12 lb/3.5–5.5 kg for a Christmas dinner.

- Allow 2–3 lb/1–1.5 kg of turkey on the bone per person.

- Frozen turkey must be completely thawed before cooking starts. Check the instructions on the packaging.

- Any neck or giblets inside should be removed.

- Wash the prepared turkey, both inside and out, in cold water and allow to drain.

- Rub the skin with butter or olive oil and then season lightly with salt and pepper.

- Lay several rashers of fatty, streaky bacon over the breast and then cover the turkey with foil. This can form a good lid over the roasting tin, or the turkey can be placed on foil, which is then folded and crimped over the top of the turkey.

- Place the meat in a roasting tin on the middle shelf of a hot oven, gas mark 7, 425°F, 220°C.

- After 30 minutes turn the heat down to moderate, gas mark 3, 325°F, 160°C for 2½–3 hours.

- Then turn the heat up to gas mark 6, 400°F, 200°C, and remove the foil and bacon for the final 30 minutes.

- Baste the turkey with its own juices several times in these final 30 minutes.

- To check to see if the bird is cooked run a skewer through the thickest thigh meat. The juice should be golden, with no trace of pink. The juices that run out of the body cavity should also be clear, not pink.

- The cooked turkey should then be allowed to relax in a warm place for 30 minutes before serving.

- We have a family of 7 for Christmas and purchase a 14 lb/6.5 kg fresh turkey. This is cooked for 40 minutes at the initial high temperature, for 3½ hours at the lower temperature, and then for 40 minutes, for the final crisping of the skin without foil.

Citrus and Pine Kernel Turkey

Serves 4
2 oranges
1 lemon or lime
4 turkey or chicken breasts
1 small onion, chopped
1 oz/25 g pine kernels
a sprig of fresh tarragon or 2 teaspoons dried tarragon
1 glass white wine
freshly ground black pepper

- Wash the fruit and grate the rind. Squeeze the juice.

- Put the turkey/chicken breasts into a shallow dish.

- Sprinkle with the onion and pine kernels.

- Mix the tarragon, wine, orange rind and juice and lemon or lime rind, together.

- Add pepper and pour over the turkey.

- Cover and cook in the oven at gas mark 6, 400°F, 200°C for 30–45 minutes.

Variations

- Use papaya or pineapple juice in place of the orange rind and juice.

Spaghetti Marrow Bolognese

Serves 4
1 spaghetti marrow
1 onion, chopped
4 oz/100 g mushrooms, sliced
herbs or seasoning to taste
1 clove garlic, crushed
olive oil
1 lb/450 g minced beef
4 oz/100 g grated hard cheese

- Bake the spaghetti marrow whole for 2 hours at gas mark 3, 325°F, 160°C.

- While it is cooking, fry the onion, mushrooms, herbs and garlic gently in the olive oil.

- Add the mince.

- Fry for 5–10 minutes, making sure the meat is cooked through.

- Then add a little hot water and simmer gently for a further 20 minutes.

- Split the marrow and extract the spaghetti-like inside.

- Arrange the marrow on plates and pile the meat sauce on top.

- Sprinkle grated cheese over the meat and serve.

Variations

- Use minced turkey for the lowest cost.

- Add bean sprouts to the onion and mushrooms.

Tip

Grow your own spaghetti marrow.

Casserole of Heart

Per person
1 lamb's heart
1 small to medium onion, chopped
olive oil
1 carrot, chopped
4 oz/100 g swede and/or turnip, chopped
other vegetables as liked and available (parsnips, mushrooms, etc.),
  chopped
1 clove garlic, crushed
herbs (sage, parsley, thyme)

- Soak the heart in cold water for at least 2 hours, then cut off the fat and arteries and clean them under a running tap, to make sure there are no blood clots left inside.

- Preheat the oven to gas mark 4, 350°F, 180°C.

- Sauté the onion in the olive oil until translucent.

- Add the remaining vegetables and the meat, cooked whole or cut into pieces.

- Sauté for a few more minutes, then transfer to a casserole and just cover with water.

- Add the herbs.

- Cover with a lid and cook in the oven for 1½–2 hours.

Tip

Hearts make an excellent gravy, which can be used with puréed vegetables for babies.

Tangy Liver

Serves 4
1 onion
olive oil for frying
4 oz/100 g mushrooms
1 lb/450 g ox liver, cut into strips
juice and grated rind of 1 orange
4 tomatoes, quartered
herbs (rosemary, thyme, oregano)

- Skin and chop the onion, and fry gently in the olive oil until translucent.

- Add the mushrooms and fry for a further 2 minutes.

- Add the liver. Fry quickly, turning until sealed on all sides.

- Add the orange juice and rind.

- Add the tomatoes and fry just long enough to heat through.

- Sprinkle with the herbs.

- Serve with green vegetables.

Variation

- Add gooseberries and fry with the onion.

Tip

Liver should not be cooked for more than a few minutes.

Ham and Asparagus Gratin

Per person
2 slices ham
2 thick stems asparagus
2 tablespoons light olive oil
1 small onion, chopped
1 clove garlic, crushed
2 fl oz/50 ml double cream
1 tablespoon fresh mayonnaise
pinch of curry powder
2 fl oz/50 ml chicken stock
1 teaspoon chopped oregano
1 teaspoon chopped chives
Parmesan cheese

- Roll the ham around the asparagus and lay in a shallow dish.

- Heat the oil, add the onion and garlic and cook gently for 3 minutes until soft.

- Blend the cream, mayonnaise and curry powder and add to the onion and garlic, simmering gently.

- Add the chicken stock and mix thoroughly. Simmer for 1 minute.

- Add most of the herbs and pour the sauce over the ham and asparagus.

- Sprinkle with the remaining herbs and a little Parmesan cheese.

- Bake at gas mark 4, 350°F, 180°C for 20–30 minutes.

Ham and Summer Vegetables

Serves 4
2 tablespoons olive oil
1 onion, chopped
2 cloves garlic, peeled and chopped
2 sticks celery, chopped
4 rashers bacon, cut into strips
2 tablespoons fresh parsley, chopped
1 tablespoon chopped basil
½ tablespoon chopped fresh marjoram or oregano
salt and pepper to taste
1 head broccoli, broken into florets
1 lb/450 g young broad beans
8 stems asparagus (optional)
4 oz/100 g cooked ham, cut into strips
toasted pine nuts

- Heat the oil and cook the onion, garlic, celery and bacon, together with the herbs and seasoning, gently for 10 minutes, then keep warm until needed as the sauce.

- Cook the broccoli and beans in boiling water until tender.

- Cook the asparagus briefly in boiling water, if using.

- Lay the vegetables in a shallow dish.

- Make a lattice with the strips of ham on top, then pour the sauce over.

- Sprinkle with toasted pine nuts and serve.

• Nuts •

With the exception of the sweet chestnut, nuts contain very useful levels of protein and oils. They are all excellent sources of many vitamins and minerals.

Nuts can be divided into two groups. The low-protein nuts –

coconut, sweet chestnut, hazelnut and pecan – can be eaten with a starch meal or a protein meal, but the high-protein nuts – almonds, Brazil nuts, cashew nuts, peanuts (groundnuts), pine nuts and pistachios – should only be eaten with a protein meal.

Coconut is also high in fat, and is a good source of many minerals and fibre. It can be used in both sweet and savoury dishes, and as a snack.

Hazelnuts can eaten fresh or lightly roasted and are a good source of minerals and vitamins.

Pecan nuts are lower in protein than most nuts, and can be used to flavour bread and cakes, or used in savoury nut dishes.

Walnuts are another good source of many minerals, and walnut oil is high in poly-unsaturates.

Almonds can be eaten whole or ground into a flour for use in cakes and starch-free breads. They should not be eaten in large quantities.

Brazil nuts have the highest fat level of any nut except pecans. Eat whole or add to savoury dishes and starch-free salads.

Cashew nuts have to be roasted and shelled by hand before sale, to remove caustic fluid that covers the nut. They are high in fat, protein and minerals. They can be eaten as a snack, made into a protein bread or added to savoury dishes.

Peanuts are legumes rather than nuts. They have high protein and fat levels. Ground peanuts can be used as a substitute for butter or other fats in baking.

Pine nuts can be eaten as snacks, added to savoury dishes or salads.

Pistachios are used to flavour sweets or eaten as a snack. They are an excellent source of iron.

	protein	starch+sugar	fat	calcium/100g
Almond	17%	19.5%	54%	* * * * *
Brazil nut	16%	10.9%	66%	* * * *
Cashew	20%	29.3%	45%	* * * *
Coconut	4%	11%	38%	* * *
Hazelnut	7.5%	16.7%	62%	* * * *
Peanut	30%	18.6%	40–50%	* * * *
Pecan	4.5%	14.6%	71%	* * * *
Pine nut	31.1%	11.6%	47.4%	–
Pistachio	22%	19%	53%	* * *
Walnut	12%	15%	60%	* * * *

*Precise calcium figures unavailable * – * * * * * indicates low to high calcium content.*

Hazelnut Loaf

Serves 4
2 onions, chopped
2–3 tablespoons olive oil
2 garlic cloves, crushed
½ teaspoon coriander seeds, crushed, or ground coriander
4 oz/100 g carrots, grated
1 glass red wine
2 tablespoons tomato purée
4 oz/100 g hazelnuts, coarsely chopped
1 tablespoon chopped parsley
salt and freshly ground black pepper to taste

- Fry the onion gently in the oil (this can be done in the microwave, using full power for 1 minute).

- Add the garlic and coriander. Stir in the carrots, wine and tomato purée and simmer for 5 minutes (2 minutes in the microwave).

- Mix in the nuts, parsley and seasoning, turn into an oven-proof glass loaf dish.

- Bake at gas mark 4, 350°F, 180°C for 46–45 minutes.

- Serve hot or cold.

Variations

- Cook at full power in the microwave for 10–12 minutes (do not allow to overcook – it should be still slightly moist when removed).

- Use grated apple in place of the carrot.

- Add grated cheese to the mixture.

- Use cashew nuts instead of hazelnuts and creamed horse-radish sauce instead of the tomato purée.

Chestnut and Herb Loaf

Serves 4
1 onion, finely chopped
2 tablespoons olive oil
2 cloves garlic, crushed
8 oz/225 g chestnut purée
1 tablespoon chopped parsley
1 tablespoon chopped fresh herbs (sage, thyme, rosemary)
6 oz/175 g carrots, grated
2 eggs, beaten
salt and freshly ground black pepper to taste

- Fry the onion gently in the oil for 2–3 minutes (1 minute in microwave).

- Add the garlic and fry for further minute (½ minute in microwave).

- Stir in all remaining ingredients and turn into an ovenproof glass bowl.

- Bake in a conventional oven at gas mark 4, 350°F, 180°C, for 40–45 minutes or in the microwave for 12 minutes.

- Leave to stand for 5 minutes before serving.

- Serve hot or cold. Accompany with spicy mayonnaise (see page 219).

Variation

- This recipe is ideal for those who do not like the crunchiness of chopped nuts. If you want a crunchy texture, add 3 oz/ 75 g each of chopped walnuts and hazelnuts.

Vegetable Nut Gratin

Serves 4
2 onions, sliced
2 tablespoons olive oil
2 cloves garlic, crushed
12 oz/350 g courgettes, sliced
6 oz/175 g carrots, sliced
1 tablespoon chopped parsley
½ tablespoon chopped rosemary
1 teaspoon chopped thyme
salt and freshly ground black pepper to taste
6 oz/175 g mixed nuts (cashew nuts halved, hazelnuts whole, Brazil/
   walnuts in pieces)
2 oz/50 g pine kernels
4 large tomatoes, skinned and sliced
¼ pint/150 ml skimmed milk
4 oz/100 g Cheddar cheese, grated

- Fry the onions gently in the oil for 2–3 minutes, then add the garlic, courgettes, carrots, herbs and seasoning. Cook for a further 5 minutes.

- Add most of the nuts, retaining some for the topping. Chop these more finely.

- Put half the mixture into a pie dish and cover with the tomatoes. Add the rest of the mixture.

- Heat the milk and stir in half the cheese. Simmer for a few minutes, then pour over the mixture in the dish.

- Sprinkle with the chopped nuts and remaining cheese. Bake at gas mark 4, 35°F, 180°C, for 30 minutes.

- Serve hot.

Chinese Cashew Stir-Fry

Serves 4
10 oz/275 g packet tofu
2 onions, sliced
2 oz/50 g carrots, thinly sliced
2 tablespoons olive oil
6 oz/175 g mushrooms, sliced
4 medium tomatoes, skinned and sliced
1 small can pineapple pieces
2 tablespoons soy sauce
1 tablespoon cider vinegar or lemon juice
1 tablespoon peanut butter
¼ pint/150 ml chicken or vegetable stock
2 oz/50 g chopped nuts (any kind)
2 oz/50 g chopped dried apricots
salt and freshly ground black pepper to taste
3 oz/75 g toasted cashew nuts

- Drain the tofu and set aside.
- Fry the onions and carrots in the oil in a large pan until the onions are soft. Stir in the mushrooms and tomatoes and cook for a further 5 minutes.
- Stir in the remaining ingredients, except for the tofu and cashew nuts. Simmer gently until the mixture thickens.
- Cut the tofu into cubes and stir into the mixture. Cover and simmer until cooked through.
- Turn into a casserole dish and sprinkle with the cashew nuts.
- Serve with fresh bean sprouts, raw or cooked in boiling water for 1 minute.

Variations

- Chicken can be used in this dish instead of tofu. Cut two large breasts into strips and fry with the onion.
- The soy sauce, peanut butter, cider vinegar or lemon juice and pineapple juice may need adjusting according to taste – it is best to add them gradually as desired.

Chestnuts with Brussels Sprouts

Serves 4
1 lb/450 g Brussels sprouts
8 oz/225 g fresh or dried chestnuts
2 oz/50 g flaked almonds, toasted
1 tablespoon chopped thyme

- If using dried chestnuts, soak them overnight. Drain.
- Simmer the sprouts and chestnuts for 10 minutes.
- Serve in a bowl, sprinkled with the almonds and thyme.

• Protein Savoury Sauces •

Pesto

This is a tradition Italian sauce for serving with protein or vegetable dishes.

Serves 4
2 oz/50 g basil leaves
6 garlic cloves, peeled and chopped
2 oz/50 g pine nuts
4 oz/100 g grated Parmesan cheese
8 fl oz/250 ml olive oil
salt and freshly ground black pepper to taste

- Purée the basil, garlic, pine nuts and cheese with half the olive oil and any seasoning until they form a paste.
- Beat in the remaining olive oil more slowly.
- Toss the chosen vegetables in the sauce and serve.

Variations

- Replace the pine nuts with cashew or pistachio nuts.
- Replace the Parmesan cheese with any well-flavoured cheese.
- Use other fresh herbs. Try chervil, chives, coriander, dill, lovage, savory or tarragon.

Tapenade

A traditional French sauce for serving with protein or vegetable dishes.

Serve 4
2 oz/50 g capers, drained
6 garlic cloves, peeled and chopped
6 oz/175 g olives, stoned
2 oz/50 g anchovy fillets
freshly ground black pepper to taste
4 fl oz/120 ml olive oil

- Purée the first five ingredients with half the olive oil until they form a paste.

- Beat in the remaining olive oil more slowly.

- Serve with crudités or hard-boiled eggs.

Blue Cheese Dressing

A simple cheese dressing for serving with green or mixed salads.

Serves 4
2 oz/50 g blue cheese (Danish blue, Cambozola, etc.)
5 oz/150 g plain Greek yogurt
1 tablespoon fresh tarragon, chopped

- Crumble the cheese into the yogurt, followed by the tarragon, or use a liquidizer to mix all the ingredients together.

- Do not keep for longer than two days in the refrigerator.

Blue Cheese and Walnut Sauce

Serve with any protein or vegetable dish.

Serves 4
4 oz/100 g soft blue cheese (Cambozola is ideal)
1 oz/200 g tub soft cream cheese
4 oz/100 g tub fromage frais
2 oz/50 g basil leaves or ½ teaspoon dried basil
1 oz/25 g parsley or ½ teaspoon dried parsley
1 small glass red wine
1 dessertspoon walnut oil
½ teaspoon ground coriander
2 oz/50 g chopped walnuts

- Melt the blue cheese gently, either in a saucepan or in a microwave (30 seconds).

- Blend all the ingredients except the nuts together in a bowl or blender.

- Add the nuts and heat the mixture gently, until almost at boiling point. Do not allow to boil.

- Pour over cooked mixed vegetables (broccoli, sweetcorn, root vegetables, cauliflower, etc.).

- Sprinkle with more herbs or some Parmesan cheese and serve at once.

Variations

- Serve in individual ovenproof gratin dishes and brown under the grill.

- Use as a warm or cold dip with raw vegetables – carrot sticks, cauliflower florets, celery, courgette sticks, etc.

Shropshire Blue cheese and Walnut Sauce

Serve with any protein or vegetable dish.

Serves 4
4 oz/100 g Shropshire Blue cheese, crumbled
8 oz/225 g cream cheese
2 tablespoons red wine or port
4 tablespoons milk
1 tablespoon chopped parsley
3 oz/75 g walnuts, chopped

- Blend all the ingredients except the nuts together in a bowl or blender.

- Add the nuts and heat the mixture gently, until almost at boiling point.

- Pour over cooked mixed vegetables and serve.

Variations

- Use as a warm or cold dip with raw vegetables, as in Blue Cheese and Walnut Sauce (see page 212). If using it cold, you do not need to heat it through first.

- Substitute Stilton or Gorgonzola for the Shropshire Blue cheese.

Marjoram Pesto

Serve with any protein or vegetable dish.

Serves 4
2 oz/50 g pine nuts
2 oz/50 g fresh marjoram, stalks included
1 clove garlic, peeled and crushed
2 oz/50 g Parmesan cheese, grated
1 tablespoon lime juice
salt to taste
8 tablespoons extra virgin olive oil
1 tablespoon sesame oil
extra pine nuts

- Blend everything except the oils, extra pine nuts and Parmesan in a bowl or blender, until not too smooth. Add the oil slowly and then blend until smooth. Do not blend for too long.

- Pour over cooked mixed vegetables.

- Top with the extra pine nuts and grated Parmesan and toast under the grill.

Variations

- Use pecans or walnuts instead of pine nuts.

Brie Sauce on Vegetables

Serve with any protein or vegetable dish.

Serves 4
1 small onion, chopped
1 tablespoon olive oil
1 glass white wine
4 tablespoons fromage frais or Greek yogurt
4 oz/100 g blue Brie or Cambozola
salt and freshly ground black pepper to taste
approx. 1 lb/450 g cooked vegetables, chopped (e.g. broccoli and sweetcorn)
2 tablespoons pine nuts

- Gently fry the onion in the oil until soft.

- Add the wine and fromage frais/yogurt and bring gently to a simmer. Do not boil.

- Simmer for 3 minutes, then add cheese and seasoning.

- Pour over the cooked vegetables in a gratin dish, sprinkle with pine nuts and toast briefly under the grill.

Sour Cream Sauce and Dip

Serve with any protein or vegetable dish.

Serves 4
¼ pint/150 ml sour cream
1 small onion, chopped
1 large garlic clove, peeled and chopped
salt and freshly ground black pepper to taste
chives to garnish

- Mix all the ingredients except the chives together.

- Sprinkle with chives and serve with crudités or as a sauce.

Variations

- Add 2 oz/50 g any blue cheese and the juice of one lemon.

- Add 4 oz/100 g finely chopped celery.

- Add a selection of fresh herbs to the dip.

- Use cottage cheese in place of the sour cream.

- Use full-fat yogurt in place of the sour cream.

Horseradish Sauce

A traditional sauce to serve with roast beef, beef stews or smoked fish.

Serves 4
2 oz/50 g fresh horseradish
2 teaspoons vinegar
salt to taste
¼ pint/150 ml double cream

- Grate the fresh horseradish and mix with the vinegar and salt.

- Whip the cream and then fold into the mixture.

- Refrigerate until ready to serve.

Hollandaise Sauce

A traditional rich sauce to serve with vegetables, fish or eggs. This sauce should be used freshly made and should not be kept.

Note that the egg yolks are not cooked.

Serves 4
6 oz/175 g butter
1½ fl oz/40 ml water
3 egg yolks
salt and pepper to taste
juice of ½ lemon

- Melt the butter in a heavy pan and allow to cool until just warm but still liquid.

- Warm the water until tepid and then blend the egg yolks, water, salt and pepper in a blender for about 10 seconds.

- Add the warm butter gradually, blending continuously. The sauce should thicken.

- Stir in the lemon juice and serve.

Variations

- Caper sauce, for boiled fish: add 2 teaspoons of capers.

- Mousseline sauce, for fish or boiled vegetables: add 4 fl oz/ 120 ml whipped cream before serving.

Oil-less Mayonnaise

A mayonnaise for salad and protein dishes. Keep refrigerated and use within a couple of days.

Note that the egg is not fully cooked.

Serves 4
2 teaspoons sugar
1 teaspoon freshly ground mustard seed or mustard powder
2 tablespoons vinegar
2 tablespoons water
1 egg
salt to taste

- Whisk all the ingredients together and then stir continuously in a double boiler over the heat until the mayonnaise has thickened. It should not be boiled.

Spicy Mayonnaise

Serves 4
3 tablespoons mayonnaise
1 tablespoon creamed horseradish
1 teaspoon paprika
1 crushed garlic clove

- Blend all the ingredients together and serve over hard-boiled eggs or salad.

- Sprinkle with a pinch of paprika or fresh chopped herbs.

Onion Gravy

This gravy should not be used with a starch meal, such as roast potatoes, if it contains protein from the meat juices.

Serves 4
2 large onions, finely chopped
4 oz/100 g mushrooms, chopped
2 tablespoons olive oil
1 teaspoon mixed herbs
1 pint/600 ml hot water or meat juices
1 glass red wine (optional)

- Fry the onions and mushrooms gently in the oil until soft.

- Add the herbs and hot water/meat juices.

- Add the wine, if using.

- Cover with a lid and simmer for 20 minutes, then remove the lid and allow to simmer until reduced and thickened.

Hot Coconut Sauce

Serves 4
4 oz/100 g coconut, fresh or desiccated
1 medium onion
¼ pint/150 ml milk
½ teaspoon chilli powder (to taste)
juice of 1 lemon

- Finely chop the coconut and onion.

- Mix all the ingredients together and cook very gently until the onion is soft.

- This sauce can also be served without cooking.

Mint Sauce

A tasty sauce to serve with roast lamb.

Serves 4
½ oz/15 g fresh mint, apple mint or spearmint leaves
4 fl oz/120 ml plain yogurt

- Chop the fresh young mint leaves finely.

- Add the yogurt and leave to stand for 30 minutes. Stir occasionally.

• Protein Sweets •

Summer Fruit

Serves 4
1 lb/450 g mixed ripe blackcurrants, gooseberries, raspberries or other soft fruit of any kind
1–2 oz/25–50 g honey
1 lb/450 g yogurt

- Simmer the fruit and honey gently in a little water until the fruit is soft but still whole. Cooking in a microwave avoids the need to add extra water.

- Whip half the fruit into the yogurt.

- Serve the remaining fruit with the yogurt whip.

Variations

- St Clements' or Winter Pudding – use oranges, with the membrane removed from their segments, sweet red grapefruit and apple.

- Add a little lemon juice.

Apricot Whip

Serves 4
8 oz/225 g dried apricots, soaked if necessary
1 dessertspoon honey
5 oz/150 g yogurt
2 egg whites
flaked almonds

- Cook the apricots with the honey in a little water until soft.

- Allow to cool, then blend with the yogurt in a liquidizer.

- Beat the egg whites until stiff, then fold into the apricot and yogurt purée.

- Pile into glass dishes and sprinkle with flaked almonds.

Variations

- Adjust the amount of yogurt to suit your own taste.

- Add a dessertspoon of apricot liqueur.

Apple Pudding

Serves 4
1 lb/450 g cooking apples
1 oz/25 g butter
1 oz/25 g molasses
2 oz/50 g ground almonds
1 egg

- Peel and core the apples and cook with the minimum of water (or microwave with no added water).

- Cream the butter and molasses together and then beat in the almonds.

- Beat the egg on its own and then beat into the butter mixture.

- Spread the cooked apple in a shallow pie dish and then cover with the butter mixture.

- Cook in a preheated oven, gas mark 4, 350°F, 180°C, for 25–35 minutes or until lightly set and the top is golden brown.

- Serve hot or cold with ice cream, whipped cream or yogurt.

Lemon Cream

Prepare in the morning for an evening meal.

Serves 4
½ oz/15 g gelatine
4 fl oz/120 ml very hot water
3 oz/75 g honey
juice of 2 lemons
2 eggs, separated
½ pint/300 ml full-fat milk

- Sprinkle the powdered gelatine over the water and stir until it dissolved.

- Add the honey and stir until all is dissolved. Allow to cool until only warm.

- Add the juice from the lemons.

- Beat the yolks and then stir into the warm solution of gelatine and honey.

- Stir the milk into the mixture, keeping it warm over a gentle heat.

- Remove the mixture from the heat.

- Beat the egg whites and fold these into the mixture.

- Pour into a serving bowl and place in the fridge until set.

❦ CHAPTER 11 ❦
Vegetable Recipes

Eat a wide range of vegetables every week. They are all good sources of potassium salts (the alkali ash noted by Dr Hay).

Vegetables should be obtained as fresh as possible and, with the exception of onions and potatoes, should be washed and dried immediately. They should then be stored in a cold, dark room and used as soon as possible. Much of the vitamin content will be lost after only a few hours' wilting in the light at room temperature.

Eat the most tender vegetables raw or cook them for the minimum time by steaming. They will thereby retain their best flavours. If you must boil vegetables, boil the water before adding the vegetables, use the minimum quantity of water and use the cooking liquid in a sauce. The liquid often contains more vitamins and minerals than the vegetables after boiling. Baked vegetables should be brushed with olive oil before placing in a preheated oven.

Do not use bicarbonate of soda when cooking vegetables. It destroys some of the vitamins completely.

Salt should not be added to cooking water – simply use a small quantity just before serving. Steamed vegetables can also be seasoned by tossing them in a tablespoon of olive oil immediately before serving.

Alfalfa is useful for sprouting for salads. It is rich in vitamins and minerals, but should not be eaten in large quantities.

Amaranth spinach is much more nutritious than lettuce. It can be cooked briefly by stir-frying or steaming.

Globe artichokes are prepared by trimming the sharp points of the leaves and breaking the stalk away from the base. The whole artichoke needs to be simmered for 45 minutes. It will need a plate on top of it to make sure it doesn't float! Drain the artichokes upside-down before serving.

The fleshy base of each leaf is eaten, as is the fleshy base, but the bud itself – the choke – is discarded.

Asparagus is cooked in the simplest way by boiling, with the bunch of stems standing upright in the pan so that the tops are steamed. The flavour of asparagus is so delicate that it doesn't require a sauce.

Aubergines should be firm, heavy and shiny. Slice thinly and then sprinkle with salt to draw out the bitter flavour. After 30 minutes the salt should be washed off and the slices dried with a clean cloth. The prepared slices can then be stewed or baked, but tend to absorb too much fat if fried so don't use more oil than the following recipes suggest.

Beans: runner beans, when fresh, should be long and thin and should snap cleanly when bent. They are best cooked by simmering in water for 10–15 minutes. They can be sliced but fewer nutrients are lost if they are cooked whole. **French beans** should be firm but thin, without fully formed seeds. Cook whole by simmering for 10–15 minutes. **Broad beans** should be eaten fresh before they have grown to full size. Thumb-nail size is best. Young beans require only 10 minutes boiling but mature beans need 20 minutes and are better used for soups and stews.

Beetroot will bleed if cut before cooking. The leaves should be removed by twisting. The roots need simmering for 20–30 minutes until soft, when the skins can be removed by rubbing. They can be baked for 35 minutes at gas mark 4, 350°F, 180°C. They are excellent served hot or cold. Beetroot also makes an excellent thickener for soups when puréed.

Young beetroot leaves are an excellent addition to a salad.

Brussels sprouts are easily overcooked. They need only be boiled for 7–8 minutes before draining and serving.

Cabbage, like all brassicas, can be eaten raw. This means that it should also be cooked for the shortest possible time, and served immediately. Cover the leaves with the minimum of water or steam them for 10–15 minutes. Longer cooking destroys both the texture and the food value.

Carrots should be washed if home-grown and no insecticides have been used, but bought carrots should be peeled to remove the surface layer with its insecticide residues. They can be grated raw for a salad or cut into thin sticks for a dip. Young carrots take 10 minutes to cook, and whole, mature carrots slightly longer. Grated carrot is also a useful addition to bread or cakes. They are the most nutritious of the hardy root crops.

Cauliflower and **broccoli** can also be eaten raw, so keep cooking to a minimum. If the stems are split it will speed up cooking. Steam if possible, or boil for 15 minutes.

Celeriac provides an excellent celery flavour for soups and stews but is not suitable for salads.

Celery is excellent raw with a salad or cooked by steaming for 15 minutes. The palest stems are best, and dark green stems have a bitter taste.

Courgettes can be eaten raw while small, or boiled for 2 minutes before draining. They can also be steamed. Larger courgettes can be cut into cubes and used in stews.

Cucumber is normally served sliced, raw in salads, but it can also be steamed or boiled for 2 minutes.

Garlic should be used fresh and cooked as little as possible for the strongest flavour. Add towards the end of the cooking period for most meat, fish and vegetable dishes.

Leeks are one of the hardiest vegetables for eating through the winter. The darkest green portions of the leaves should be discarded and the roots cut away from the base of the stem. If you cut up from just above the base to the top of the leaves, any soil can be washed out of the leaves without their becoming tangled. Leeks need simmering in water or wine for 15 minutes.

Lettuce provides a useful source of vitamin A, but few other nutrients. It can be eaten hot in soups but its main use is in salads.

Marrows can be baked in the oven. The time needed depends on their size. They can be cut into chunks and boiled for 2 minutes or used in stews.

Mushrooms can be eaten raw in salads, or cooked with stews and soups.

Onions must have the brown skin removed before cooking. Slice thinly to serve raw in salad, or fry in the minimum quantity of olive oil for 10 minutes. Boil whole onions for 20 minutes or bake in the oven for 30 minutes.

Parsnips should be peeled to remove the skin and then cut into large chunks. They can be boiled for 15–20 minutes or sprinkled with olive oil and roasted in the oven.

Peas are best raw in salads when young and fresh. Older peas need boiling for 15 minutes.

Peppers contain the most vitamin C when large and red. They can be sliced and, with the seeds removed, eaten raw. They can also be simmered for 10 minutes.

Radishes make an excellent salad vegetable.

Sweet corn can be baked in their husks, but normally the husks are removed and the cob cooked in boiling water: 5 minutes for the youngest corn, 20 minutes if they are very mature.

Tomatoes are most nutritious eaten raw, but they make an excellent sauce for many protein or starch dishes.

Turnips and **swedes** need peeling. When they are mature, the skin is thick and the flesh is very hard, so take care when cutting them! Cut the flesh into chunks and boil for 20 minutes until soft, or grate the root and stir-fry with a spoonful of olive oil until soft and tender. The temperature should not be high enough for the turnip to brown.

	protein	starch	sugar	fat	calcium/100 g
aubergines	0.9%	0.2%	2.0%	0.4%	10mg
beans, runner	1.2%	0.3%	2%	0.5%	29mg
beetroot	2.3%	0.7%	8.8%	0.1%	29mg
cabbage	1.7%	0.1%	4%	0.4%	52mg
carrots	0.6%	0.3%	4.6%	0.4%	24mg
celery	0.5%		0.9%	0.2%	41mg
courgettes	1.8%	0.1%	1.7%	0.4%	25mg
cucumber	0.7%	0.1%	1.4%	0.1%	18mg
lettuce	0.8%		1.7%	0.5%	28mg
mushrooms	1.8%	0.2%	0.2%	0.5%	6mg
onions	1.2%	2.3%	5.6%	0.2%	25mg
parsnips	1.6%	7%	5.9%	1.2%	50mg
peas	6.0%	7%	2.7%	0.9%	35mg
turnips	0.6%	0.1%	1.9%	0.2%	45mg

• Sprouting Seeds •

Sprouting your own seeds improves the nutritional value of the food and provides fresh green food all year round. The amounts of vitamins A and C are increased and the digestibility of the seed improved.

You should not use those seeds intended for use as garden or agricultural seed, as these have often been treated with fungicides.

Place the seeds to be sprouted in a large glass jar and soak them in six times their volume of cold water overnight. Cover the top of the jar with a muslin cloth to act as a strainer and drain the seeds. Now rinse them through the muslin several times and drain again.

Shake the seeds to spread them out and place in the jar in a well-ventilated, warm, dark place, still with the muslin cover in place. Rinse the seeds again in fresh water three times a day or more, leaving them drained each time.

It takes 3–5 days for the sprouts to grow to their best size, but this is a matter of individual taste. If the seeds are grown for too long, or too much light is allowed in, they may become bitter.

The well-rinsed sprouts can be kept in the refrigerator for a couple of days if necessary.

Sprouted seeds can be used in salads, coleslaws, for sandwich fillings, soups and stews.

Suitable seeds for sprouting include mung beans, dried peas, whole lentils, brassica seed, radish seed, wheat grain, fenugreek and alfalfa.

Warning

Sorghum sprouts should not be used, as they are very poisonous. Soy sprouts should be cooked before eating and not used fresh in salads. Alfalfa sprouts do not cook well.

Sesame, Pumpkin and Sunflower Seeds

These seeds are lower in fat and higher in protein than nuts. Sesame in particular is an excellent source of calcium. The fat is mostly polyunsaturated. Sesame seed, ground into a paste, is called tahini.

All these seeds can be eaten toasted as snacks or can be used to make starch-free pastry for flans.

• Salads •

Coleslaw

Coleslaw can be based on a wide variety of raw vegetables and the quantities are not particularly important, as long as you have plenty of variety. Vary the proportion of ingredients as you require.

Serves 4
2 eating apples
6 oz/175 g hard white cabbage
2 oz/50 g celery
2 oz/50 g onion
4 oz/100 g carrot
1 oz/25 g chopped parsley
1 teaspoon caraway seed
1 tablespoon olive oil
1 tablespoon lemon juice
salt to taste

- Core and dice the apples.
- Slice the cabbage as thinly as possible.
- Slice the celery and onion.
- Grate the carrot.
- Mix all the ingredients together, and mix again before serving.

Greek Salad

Serves 4
4 medium tomatoes
½ cucumber
1 medium onion
2 tablespoons olive oil
1 tablespoon lemon juice
6 oz/175 g feta cheese
10 black olives
pinch fresh basil

- Thinly slice the tomatoes, cucumber and onion and mix with the olive oil and lemon juice.

- Cut the cheese into small cubes and place on top.

- Scatter the olives on top.

- Sprinkle freshly chopped basil over the salad.

Celery and Apple Salad

Serves 4
1 head of celery, sliced
4 dessert apples, cored and sliced
2 oz/50 g walnuts, chopped
3 tablespoons Sesame Dressing (see page 00)
1 tablespoon sesame seeds, toasted

- Slice the celery and apple into a bowl, mix in the chopped walnuts and pour over the dressing.

- Sprinkle with sesame seeds just before serving.

Spicy Broad Bean and Pine Kernel Salad

Serves 4
1 lb/450 g shelled broad beans, small and fresh
1 teaspoon olive oil
juice of ½ lemon
3 tablespoons yogurt
4 tablespoons spicy mayonnaise (see page 219)
1 tablespoon fresh mint, chopped
1 tablespoon fresh herbs, chopped (basil, oregano, chives, thyme, parsley, marjoram in any combination)
1 oz/25 g pine kernels

- Cook the beans until just tender, then drain and toss them with the olive oil and lemon juice while still hot. Leave to cool.

- Mix together the yogurt, mayonnaise and most of the herbs.

- Mix with the beans and pine kernels.

- Sprinkle with the remaining herbs and serve.

Fennel Salad

Serves 4
2 fennel bulbs
¼ teaspoon fennel seeds
4 tablespoons French dressing with herbs (see page 245)
fresh mint, chopped

- Clean and peel the fennel bulbs, then grate them coarsely.

- Crush the fennel seeds and combine with the grated fennel and French dressing.

- Sprinkle with mint and serve.

Salads: Further Suggestions

Choose ingredients that give a range of textures, flavours and colours. There are so many salad combinations possible that every salad can offer new variety. Fresh herbs add their own flavours. Some of the best salads are produced by selecting a good mix of all the salad ingredients available. This is not an area where you need to follow recipes!

Many vegetables can be served in salad, either cooked or raw. Uncooked vegetables should be crunchy. If they seem slightly tough, try dropping them in boiling water briefly to blanch them. Strongly flavoured vegetables can be marinated in a sauce for up to two hours, but they do not improve after 12 hours.

Most green leaf salads are best when the leaves are young and fresh, developing bitter flavours as they get older.

The simplest dressing is made of lemon juice and olive oil. Toss the salad in a tablespoon of each.

Most dressings are best applied just before serving, at room temperature.

Traditional salad combinations

- Lettuce with a simple dressing.

- Lamb's lettuce and beetroot.

- Tomato and basil.

- Avocado and tomato or mint.

- Grated carrot dressed with yogurt and sprinkled with cumin.

- Sliced raw mushroom dressed with olive oil.

- Celery, walnut and apple.

- Chinese cabbage.

- Chicory greens dressed with lemon juice.

Recipes

- Cucumber sliced in yogurt and sprinkled with fresh mint.
- Courgettes.
- Beetroot greens and lettuce.
- Sprouted seeds.
- Onion and radish.

Cooked vegetables, served cold in salad:
- Green beans and tomato.
- Peas and asparagus.
- Spring turnip and raw onions.
- Cauliflower and carrot.

• Vegetable Dishes •

Ratatouille

Serves 4
1 medium aubergine, sliced
3 cloves garlic, chopped or crushed
1 lb/450 g courgettes, sliced
1 red pepper, seeded and sliced into rings
1 green pepper, seeded and sliced into rings
1 lb/450 g large tomatoes, skinned and thickly sliced
1 dessertspoon chopped basil
1 dessertspoon chopped marjoram
salt and freshly ground black pepper
6 tablespoons olive oil
1 glass white wine

- Slice the aubergine thinly and then sprinkle liberally with salt. Leave to stand for 30 minutes and then wash well, to rinse off all the salt, and blot the slices dry with a clean cloth.

- Mix all the vegetables and herbs together in a large, shallow oven dish and sprinkle with salt and pepper.

- Drizzle the oil and wine over the top.

- Roast in the oven at gas mark 5, 375°F, 190°C, for 20–30 minutes until cooked.

- Serve hot or cold.

Variations

- Top with pine nut kernels.

- For a protein dish, top with sliced mozzarella or grated Parmesan cheese.

- For a starch dish, top with sliced potatoes.

Vegetarian Moussaka

Serves 4
8 oz/225 g aubergine
salt
4 oz/100 g red lentils
½ teaspoon mixed herbs
¼ pint/150 ml water
4 oz/100 g tomatoes
1 clove garlic, crushed
1 onion, chopped
2 tablespoons olive oil
1 egg
6 oz/175 g soft cheese or fromage frais

- Slice the aubergine thinly and then sprinkle liberally with salt. Leave to stand for 30 minutes and then wash well, to rinse off all the salt, and blot the slices dry with a clean cloth.

- Simmer the lentils and herbs in the water for 30 minutes.

- Fry the aubergines, tomatoes, garlic and onion in the olive oil until soft.

- Mix the cooked lentils with the rest of the vegetables and place in an ovenproof bowl.

- Beat the egg and cheese together and pour over the top of the vegetables.

- Cook in a preheated oven at gas mark 6, 400°F, 200°C and bake for 20–25 minutes.

Indian Chilli Tomatoes

Serves 4
1 onion, chopped
2 tablespoons olive oil
1 lb/450 g tomatoes, sliced
½ inch/1 cm piece of fresh ginger, chopped
½ teaspoon crushed cardamom
½ teaspoon chilli powder
1 teaspoon molasses
½ teaspoon crushed coriander
2 tablespoons chopped coriander

- Fry the onion in the oil until soft.

- Add the remaining ingredients, except the molasses and fresh coriander, and simmer without covering until the mixture thickens.

- Add the molasses and cook for a further 5 minutes.

- Stir in the fresh coriander and serve.

Variations

- Use oregano or basil in place of the fresh coriander.

Herby Courgettes

Serves 4
8 spring onions, sliced
2 cloves garlic, chopped or crushed
4 tablespoons olive oil
1 lb/450 g courgettes, sliced
1 tablespoon chopped basil
1 tablespoon chopped marjoram
1 tablespoon chopped coriander
1 tablespoon pine nut kernels, toasted

- Fry the onions and garlic gently in the oil for 2 minutes.

- Add the courgettes and herbs, saving a little of each herb, and cover, cooking for 10–15 minutes until the courgettes are tender.

- Turn into a shallow dish, sprinkle with the pine nuts and remaining herbs, and serve.

Variation

- This dish can be cooked in the oven instead, at gas mark 5, 375°F, 190°C, for 20–30 minutes.

Fried Ladies' Fingers

Serves 4
8 oz/225 g okra (ladies' fingers)
salt
2 tablespoons olive oil
1 teaspoon ground coriander
1 teaspoon ground cardamom seeds
1 teaspoon paprika
8 oz/225 g Greek yogurt
1 tablespoon chopped basil or majoram

- Put the okra into a pan, sprinkle with salt, cover with water and boil for 10 minutes, until just tender.

- Drain, then pat dry with kitchen paper.

- Heat the oil and add the okra. Add the coriander and cardamom and fry gently for 5 minutes, turning occasionally.

- Mix the paprika with the yogurt and add to the pan. Heat through, stirring, but do not boil.

- Sprinkle with the basil/marjoram and serve.

Variations

- Add 2 chopped cloves or crushed garlic with the spices.

- Add chopped spring onions with the spices.

Vegetable and Fruit Curry

Serves 4
2 onions, sliced
3 tablespoons olive oil
1 teaspoon chilli powder
1 tablespoon ground coriander
1 inch/2.5 cm piece of fresh ginger, peeled and chopped
salt to taste
4 courgettes, sliced
2 carrots, sliced
1 aubergine, sliced
4 oz/100 g sweet corn
2 peaches, sliced
4 oz/100 g seedless grapes
1 eating apple, sliced
8 oz/225 g can tomatoes
4 green chillies

- Fry the onions in the oil until soft, then add the chilli powder, coriander, ginger and salt and fry for 2 minutes.

- Add the courgettes, carrots and aubergine and cook for 5 minutes, stirring occasionally.

- Add the sweet corn, fruit, tomatoes and chillies.

- Cover and simmer for 20 minutes.

- Remove the lid, simmer for a further 5 minutes until the sauce is thick, then serve with rice.

Variations

- Add cauliflower florets to the vegetables.

- Add cubed potatoes to the vegetables: there is then no need to use rice, unless a much more substantial dish is required.

Stuffed Courgettes

Serves 4
4 large courgettes
1 large onion, chopped
2 cloves garlic, chopped or crushed
2 sticks celery, chopped
2 tablespoons olive oil
6 oz/175 g chopped mushrooms
2 oz/50 g walnuts, chopped
2 oz/50 g hazelnuts, chopped
2 oz/50 g Brazil nuts, chopped
1 tablespoon tomato purée
1 tablespoon chopped basil
1 tablespoon chopped marjoram or oregano
salt and freshly ground black pepper
extra basil or marjoram

- Cook the courgettes in boiling water until just tender. Drain and set aside.

- Fry the onion, garlic and celery in the oil until soft.

- Add the mushrooms and cook for 3 minutes.

- Add the nuts, tomato purée, herbs and seasoning. Warm gently but do not allow to cook any further.

- Cut the courgettes in half lengthways, scoop out the flesh without breaking the skin, and mix it with the fried mixture.

- Replace the mixture in the courgette shells and heat under the grill.

- Sprinkle with the extra basil or marjoram and serve at once.

Variations

- The stuffed courgettes may be heated in the oven instead of under the grill.

- Use aubergines in place of courgettes. Bake in the oven at gas mark 5, 375°F/190°C, for 30 minutes instead of boiling.

Baked Fennel

Serves 4
2 fennel bulbs
½ small lemon, thinly sliced
salt and freshly ground black pepper
butter
1 oz/25 g hazelnuts, chopped and toasted lightly
chopped herbs (chives, basil, oregano)

- Trim and thickly slice the fennel bulbs. Place in boiling water and add the lemon and seasoning.

- Simmer for 15–20 minutes until tender.

- Drain and serve, sprinkled with the butter, nuts and herbs.

Tangy Cauliflower

Serves 4
1 cauliflower, broken into florets
salt and freshly ground black pepper
4–5 tablespoons olive oil
1 tablespoon balsamic vinegar
grated rind and juice of 1 orange
1 tablespoon chopped oregano

- Simmer the cauliflower in boiling seasoned water for 5 minutes. Drain.

- Mix together the oil, vinegar and rind and juice of the orange.

- Add to the cauliflower and toss gently.

- Sprinkle with the oregano and serve.

Red Cabbage with Apples

Serves 4
1 medium red cabbage, sliced
1 lb/450 g cooking apples, peeled and sliced
1 lb/450 g onions, sliced
2 cloves
2 cloves garlic, chopped or crushed
grated rind and juice of 1 orange
salt and freshly ground black pepper
¼ pts/150 ml pint red wine
¼ pts/150 ml pint red wine vinegar

- Layer the cabbage, apples and onions in a casserole dish until all have been used, placing the cloves in the middle.

- Mix the garlic, orange rind and juice, seasoning, wine and vinegar in a jug and pour over the cabbage mixture.

- Cover and cook at gas mark 3, 325°F, 160°C, for 2 hours.

Leeks with Almonds

Serves 4
8 medium leeks
salt and freshly ground black pepper
2 oz/50 g flaked almonds
herbs, chopped (basil, marjoram)

- Wash and slice the leeks. Season and simmer in boiling water for 5–10 minutes until just cooked.

- Sprinkle with the flaked almonds, toast briefly under the grill, sprinkle with the herbs and serve.

• Crudités •

Fresh, crisp sticks cut from a wide variety of fresh vegetables, or fruit, make excellent snacks or starters They can also be served with a basic herb dressing, with any meal. For a starch meal use the starch sauces on pages 152–4. For a protein meal use the protein savoury sauces on pages 210–21.

Avocado Dip

Serves 4

Mix the fresh of two ripe avocados with mayonnaise sauce (see page 219).

Ideas for crudités

- Carrot, cut into sticks.
- Red pepper (remove seeds).
- Courgettes, small, cut into sticks.
- Celery sticks.
- Cauliflower, small florets.
- Radishes, sliced.
- Mushrooms, raw, sliced.
- Spring onions.
- Apple, sliced.

• Dressings and Butters •

French Dressing with Herbs

¼ pint/150 ml olive oil
1½ tablespoons white wine vinegar
1 clove garlic, crushed
2 teaspoons soft brown sugar
1 teaspoon wholegrain mustard
1 tablespoon chives, chopped
1 tablespoon thyme, chopped
1 tablespoon mint, chopped
salt and freshly ground black pepper

- Mix all the ingredients together – a blender or food processor does this in 20 seconds.

- The dressing can be kept in a small, screw-topped jar in the refrigerator for up to a week.

Variation

- Use white wine instead of wine vinegar.

Sesame Dressing

2 tablespoons white wine vinegar
2 tablespoons sesame oil
4 tablespoons olive oil
1 teaspoon wholegrain mustard
2 teaspoons sesame seeds
2 tablespoons white or rosé wine
1 teaspoon soft brown sugar

- Mix all the ingredients together using a blender.

- The dressing can be kept in a small, screw-topped jar in the refrigerator for up to a week.

Garlic Butter

Garlic butter can be served with starch or protein meals.

4 oz/100 g butter
2 garlic cloves
salt to taste
½ oz/15 g chives

- Warm the butter slightly and then beat into a cream.

- Use a pestle and mortar, grind the garlic with the salt into a paste, and then beat into the creamed butter.

- Gently mix in the chives.

- Refrigerate until ready to serve.

Variations

- Fresh herb butter: add a teaspoon each of chopped tarragon and parsley in place of the garlic.

- Watercress butter: add a small handful of chopped watercress in place of the garlic.

- Tomato butter: add 2 teaspoons of tomato purée to the butter.

Black Butter

A traditional butter sauce to serve with fish or vegetables. It should be made immediately before serving.

4 oz/100 g butter
1 tablespoon chopped parsley
1 teaspoon capers
1 tablespoon vinegar

- Heat the butter in a heavy-bottomed pan until it becomes brown (not black). Take care as it changes very quickly

- Add the chopped parsley and capers.

- Immediately before serving stir the vinegar into the hot butter.

- Serve hot.

❦ CHAPTER 12 ❦
Fresh
Non-Starchy Fruit

Several pieces of fresh fruit should be eaten every day. If you eat a variety each week, you will never need vitamin supplements!

Apples are better eaten as the fruit than as fruit juice. Dried or fresh apple can be added to bread mixes.

Apricots are particularly rich in vitamin A, iron and potassium. Dried apricots are always available out of season and can be eaten raw or soaked for 24 hours in water to rehydrate them. They can also be chopped and added to bread or cake mixtures.

Avocados are 15 per cent fat but contain no cholesterol. They are a good source of many vitamins and potassium. They should be purchased rock-hard and ripened for several days on a warm shelf. For quicker ripening, place with a banana in a brown paper bag.

Bilberries and **cranberries** have an excellent flavour, which can be exploited by serving them with meat or fromage frais or yogurt.

Blackcurrants and **redcurrants** are an excellent source of vitamin C and iron throughout the year as they freeze so well. Serve them with yogurt or fromage frais, rather than with sugar.

Brambles (blackberries) from the hedgerow also freeze well and are another excellent source of vitamins C and E.

Carambola, or star fruit, come from an Indonesian tree. The flavour can be variable, but they provide useful amounts of vitamin C.

Citrus fruit – oranges, lemons, tangerines, grapefruits, limes – are all excellent sources of vitamin C. The fruit is far better nutritionally than the juice by itself. Best eaten raw, and useful for a snack at any time of day.

Figs have the highest protein content of any fruit. Fresh figs have the best flavour, but dried figs store well and make a useful snack. They can also be rehydrated by soaking for 12 hours and then simmering for 30 minutes.

Gooseberries are an excellent source of vitamin C, other vitamins and minerals. If left on the bush, they will ripen and become sweet, when they are really best used raw. Unripe berries can be used in fruit stews and served with yogurt or fromage frais, rather than sugar.

Grapes contain a range of minerals. The skins may also help prevent heart disease.

Guavas turn from green to yellow as they ripen. They are an excellent source of vitamin C and other vitamins and minerals.

Kiwi fruit should be eaten raw, or they can be served with yogurt. They are also an excellent source of Vitamin C.

Mangoes turn from green to yellow, and then orange or pink, as they ripen. The sticky flesh is eaten raw.

Melons are largely composed of water. There is no evidence that they are indigestible, as suggested by Dr Hay.

Peaches are a useful source of manganese. Best eaten fresh, but the stones should not be eaten.

Pears remain very hard while unripe, but soften quickly on ripening.

Pineapples should only be eaten with a protein meal, as the fresh fruit contains a protein-digesting enzyme. Fresh pineapple juice is very useful for marinating meat.

Plums can be eaten fresh, but some varieties are not very sweet and are better simmered until tender, with only a little added water.

Raspberries are easily bruised and do not travel or keep well, although they are easily frozen. Eat fresh or serve with yogurt. They are a good source of iron.

Rhubarb stalks should only be eaten in the spring. They are best if simmered, but no water should be added. Cook them in a microwave if you have one. Serve with yogurt rather than sugar to mask the sour flavour.

Strawberries are a good source of vitamins when eaten fresh. They can also be added to fruit stews.

	protein	starch	sugar	fat	calcium/100g
Apples	0.4%		11.8%	0.1%	4mg
Apricots	4%		36.5%	0.6%	73mg
Avocados	1.9%	1.4%	0.5%	19.5%	11mg
Blackcurrants and redcurrants	0.8%		5.6%		51mg
Gooseberries	0.4%	16%	2.5%	0.2%	23mg
Grapefruit	0.8%		6.8%	0.1%	23mg
Grapes	0.4%		15.4%	0.1%	23mg
Kiwi fruit	1.1%	0.3%	10.3%	0.5%	25mg
Mangoes	0.7%	0.3%	13.8%	0.2%	12mg
Melons	0.6%		6.6%	0.1%	9mg
Oranges	1.1%		8.5%	0.1%	47mg
Pears	0.3%		10%	0.1%	11mg
Plums	0.6%		8.8%	0.1%	13mg
Raspberries	1.4%		4.6%	0.3%	25mg
Strawberries	0.8%		6%	0.1%	16mg

Serving Fruit

Fresh fruit makes an excellent breakfast and lunch, or snack. It can also be eaten with protein meals.

Many traditional recipes spoil the nutritional value of fruit by adding excessive amounts of sugar (e.g. in pavlova, vacherin) or sugar syrup; or excessive amounts of fat when served in pastry, fruit fools or ice cream.

Most fruit should be served when ripe with only its own juice. A little fresh or clotted cream adds a touch of luxury. Fruit that is slightly sour can be served with yogurt, rather than having sugar added.

Fruit to be served hot is best cooked in a microwave oven, where no extra water need be added. It can also be served sautéed in a little butter.

Fruit salads can be served with the fruit thinly sliced or cubed. When a melon has been used, the fruit salad can be returned to the scooped-out melon shell for serving.

Vegetable and Fruit Juices

Extracting the juice from fruit or vegetables discards many of the nutrients and bypasses the appetite-control mechanisms. Fruit sugars in this form can produce surges in blood sugar in the same way as refined sugar.

It is far more healthy to drink water, and to eat the whole fresh fruit or vegetable!

Winter Fruit Salad

Serves 4
6 oz/175 g dried Hunza apricots
4 oz/100 g dried prunes
4 oz/100 g dried apple rings
1 pint/600 ml apple juice or ½ pint/300 ml each of orange juice and water
1 dessertspoon honey
4 cloves
cinnamon to taste
1 oz/25 g flaked almonds

- Soak the dried fruit in the fruit juice/fruit juice and water for 2 hours or overnight.

- Add the honey and cloves and sprinkle with the cinnamon.

- Bring to the boil and simmer for 10–15 minutes.

- Sprinkle with the almonds.

- Serve with cream or natural yogurt.

Variations

- For a starch winter fruit salad, use dates, figs, raisins and sultanas, and grape juice.

Apple and Bramble Pudding

Serves 4
2 cooking apples
1 lb/450 g brambles (blackberries)
4 cloves
cinnamon to taste
1 dessertspoon honey

Microwave method

- Peel, core and slice the apples.

- Mix with the brambles in a microwave-proof bowl or casserole dish.

- Add the cloves and cinnamon.

- Add the honey.

- Add water to about halfway up the fruit.

- Cook on full power for 5–8 minutes, stirring occasionally.

If you have no microwave, simmer on the hob until the fruit is cooked.

Variations

- Use marrow or pumpkin in place of the apple.

❧ CHAPTER 13 ❧
Christmas Recipes

Breakfast

Fresh fruit salad

Main meal

Avocado dip and crudités

Roast turkey
Sprouts, carrots, baked onion, cauliflower
Onion gravy

Apple and a selection of cheeses

Supper

New potatoes and salads with a pesto dressing

Christmas pudding with mincemeat sauce

Fresh fruit

Mincemeat

Serve mincemeat with either a protein or starch meal.

Makes 1 lb/450 g mincemeat
1 lemon
2 oz/50 g sultanas
2 oz/50 g raisins
2 oz/50 g currants
2 oz/50 g apples, with cores removed
2 oz/50 g suet
2 oz/50 g molasses
¼ teaspoon mixed spice
½ teaspoon ground ginger
¼ teaspoon ground nutmeg
½ teaspoon ground cinnamon
¼ ground mace
1 fl oz/30 ml brandy

- Cook the lemon, peel and all, in a little water until soft, then chop finely in a food processor.
- Put all the remaining fruit and suet in small quantities through a food processor to chop quite finely.
- Mix all the processed fruit and suet together with the lemon, molasses and spices.
- Mix in the brandy, cover the bowl and leave to stand for 24 hours. Mix again before pressing into jars.
- Keep at least 2 weeks before using.

Serve mincemeat:
- with baked apples
- with yogurt
- as a spread on bread or any of the cakes in this book
- as a hot sauce on Christmas pudding.

Christmas Pudding – starch meal

Serves 4

2 oz/50 g unsweetened tinned chestnut purée
2 oz/50 g apple, grated
2 eggs
2 fl oz/50 ml milk
1 oz/25 g rice flour
4 oz/100 g breadcrumbs
4 oz/100 g suet, grated
4 oz/100 g molasses
4 oz/100 g currants
4 oz/100 g sultanas
4 oz/100 g raisins
1 oz/25 g glacé cherries
1 tablespoon treacle
1 oz/25 g ground almonds
1 lemon, grated and squeezed
½ wine glass brandy
¼ teaspoon salt
1 teaspoon ground nutmeg
1 teaspoon ground cinnamon

- Beat the chestnut and apple to a smooth purée with the eggs and milk. This is best done in a liquidizer.
- Transfer the purée to a large mixing bowl, then gradually mix in all the remaining ingredients, stirring well.
- Place the mixture in well-greased pudding basins. They should not be over-full.
- Cover with greaseproof paper and then aluminium foil tied tightly round the top of the bowl.
- A 1 pint/600 ml basin should be steamed for 4 hours, a 2 pint/1.2 litre basin for 6 hours.
- If a pressure cooker is available, steam for 30 minutes without pressure and then for 3 hours under high pressure.
- Always check water levels when steaming for several hours.
- For the best flavour steam for 2–3 hours to reheat before serving.

Conversion Tables

Oven temperatures

gas mark ½	250°F	120°C
gas mark 1	275°F	140°C
gas mark 2	300°F	150°C
gas mark 3	325°F	160°C
gas mark 4	350°F	180°C
gas mark 5	375°F	190°C
gas mark 6	400°F	200°C
gas mark 7	425°F	220°C
gas mark 8	450°F	230°C
gas mark 9	475°F	240°C

Solid measures

ounces	grams (approx.)	grams (accurate)
1	25	28
2	50	57
3	75	85
4	100	113
5	150	142
6	175	170
7	200	198
8	225	227
9	250	255
10	275	283
11	300	312
12	350	340
13	375	368
14	400	396
15	425	425
16 (1 lb)	450	454
1½ lb	680	681
2 lb	900	910

Liquid measure

fl oz	pints	millilitres (approx.)	millilitres (accurate)
½		15	14
1		30	28
2		50	56
3		85	85
4		120	113
5	¼	150	142
6		175	170
7		200	199
8		250	227
9		275	256
10	½	300	283
15	¾	450	425
20	1	600	567
30	1½	900	851
35	1¾	1 litre	992
	2	1.1 litres	1134

1 teaspoon=1 level teaspoon=5 ml
1 tablespoon=1 level tablespoon=15 ml

Index

The words 'food combining' when they appear in sub-headings have been abbreviated to fc.

Index

Index